How to Become a Master of Persuasion

How to Become a Master of Persuasion

Establishing Value and Convincing Your Customers of It

Tony Treacy

BUSINESS EXPERT PRESS

Leader in applied, concise business books

How to Become a Master of Persuasion:
Establishing Value and Convincing Your Customers of It

Cover design by Charlene Kronstedt

Interior design by Exeter Premedia Services Private Ltd., Chennai, India

First published in 2021 by
Business Expert Press, LLC
222 East 46th Street, New York, NY 10017
www.businessexpertpress.com

ISBN-13: 978-1-63742-090-4 (paperback)
ISBN-13: 978-1-63742-091-1 (e-book)

Business Expert Press Corporate Communication Collection

Collection ISSN: 2156-8162 (print)
Collection ISSN: 2156-8170 (electronic)

First edition: 2021

10 9 8 7 6 5 4 3 2 1

Description

This book is perfect for everyone involved in sales who wants to be a better and more persuasive communicator. It is a practical guide that explains what motivates customers, how to identify the best things to talk about, how to control every pitch, and how to persuade customers to buy from you.

Keywords

pitching; presenting; business storytelling; persuading; communicating; impressing; influencing; speaking; business process; word craft

Contents

Review Quotes ix

Preface xi

Chapter 1   Why Persuasion Is at the Heart of Pitching 1

Chapter 2   Step 1—Communication Objective 9

Chapter 3   Step 2—Meeting Goal 25

Chapter 4   Step 3—Story Plan...33

Chapter 5   Case Studies 43

Chapter 6   Step 4—Content...59

Chapter 7   Step 5—Style and Language..73

Chapter 8   Step 6—Pitch and Presentation.....................................97

Chapter 9   How to Use the Six-Step Process 125

About the Author 129

Index 131

Review Quotes

"If you need to pitch for business then you really do need to read this book. Tony is a true master of both the art and science behind pitching and here he has managed to blend these into a simple, thorough, process to create compelling and winning proposals. Its practical, valuable advice and soundly based in his extensive real-world experience. Highly Recommended!"—**Nick Dunlop, Managing Director Willis Towers Watson**

"Easy to read. It really simplifies pitching and sets out a process that is practical and logically structured. The case studies are interesting and useful, and it is easy to see how businesses will improve the way they pitch if they apply what it teaches."—**David Herbinet, Global Head of Audit Mazars**

"A "go to" communications bible for everyone involved in business development and sales. It is a logical and practical guide to building effective customer-centric communication for the virtual and physical world."—**Sasha Molodtsov, Director BDO LLP**

"A perfect companion to ensuring your communication and pitching is on point and effective. The chapters flow logically through the steps you need to take to produce effective content and improve personal presentation skills. This is a great guide to mastering the art of persuasion."—**Andrew Rhodes, B2b Marketing Manager Just Park**

Preface

If you work for a company who sells products, services, and solutions to other companies, then you'll be interested in this book, because it is all about how you persuade a customer to buy from you.

The starting point is to recognize that business is doomed unless it has a regular stream of new sales. Sales are the life blood of business. Sales are the oxygen that a business needs to breathe, and if you don't have new sales, then you don't have a business, right?

So, everyone needs customers and most of us spend a lot of time and energy trying to win new customers, so our businesses can be successful, and we can make some money.

The big question is why does a customer buy from you?

Business is won when the customer thinks you have the right answers, the right products, the right people, and the right skills. This is why they buy. Whether this happens depends on your ability to persuade them.

Persuasion means inducing or leading someone to do something through reason and argument, in this case, buying something from you, and whether you persuade a customer is not a matter of chance.

Customers are persuaded when they believe what you offer is better than anyone else, which is determined by whether your pitch is compelling and whether you communicate your value brilliantly in written proposals, at meetings, and at presentations.

If pitching and persuading a customer is an essential skill, how good are you at communicating? How good is your sales pitch? How persuasive are the reasons and arguments you put to your customers, and how often do they buy?

These questions are probably even more important than they have ever been before. The global pandemic isn't over, and although some businesses have flourished, many others have struggled through shutdowns and restrictions that have limited human contact and turned normal working practices upside down.

It's as though we've all been living in a dark tunnel, and after months and months are only now moving toward the light. When we get there, when business steps out back into the light, life will change for the better as things start to return to normal. However, when the starting gun goes off, there is a key question all business leaders need to answer: Will they be ready to sprint? Will the sales and business development teams be ready to take advantage of market opportunities? Will they be able and ready to convince customers to buy from them, or will they need to prepare for the race?

So, if you think your business needs to find better ways to win new customers and if you think you could improve the way you pitch and be better and more effective communicators, then this book helps you. It is focused on helping everyone who is involved in sales or business development and teaches you how to become a Master of Persuasion.

In short, this book helps you to become a better and more persuasive communicator. It is a practical guide to help you understand a customer's goals and motivations, to identify the most relevant and important issues to talk about, to take control of every pitch situation, and to plan and then deliver proposals and presentations that will persuade your customers to buy from you.

This book is based on training courses that have been attended by hundreds of businesses over the years. It contains real-world case studies and personal insights about pitching that explain how to prepare for every step in the sales process and provides tools that will enable you to apply this knowledge immediately to your business.

As well as enhancing skills to deliver pitches and presentations, it also explains how to transfer face-to-face skills to the current work environment, where video conferencing has become the new normal.

This book helps you to:

- Understand customers' goals and motivations
- Identify the most relevant and important issues to talk about
- Predict the attitude of the audience you will be pitching to
- Learn how to write benefit-focused pitches
- Focus on the key issues that are relevant to the customer
- Work together more collaboratively and effectively as a team

- Save time producing pitch documents and presentations
- Enhance your personal impact at meetings and presentations
- Learn how to handle video conferencing more effectively individually and as a team
- Become a better and more persuasive communicator

The author, Tony Treacy, has over 35 years of experience in business. He was a marketing director for a leading accountancy firm, ran an award-winning integrated agency working with some of the largest global brands, was a director at an international graphics business, and was a specialist for a global company in the printing and publishing industry.

Since setting up his own company in 2010, Tony has been an independent consultant and business skills trainer and coach since then putting this knowledge into action.

Tony is a Fellow of the Marketing Society, an affiliate member of the Chartered Institute of Marketing, a mentor for the Business Growth Programme, a trainer for techUK, and managing director at Pitch Factory Limited, which is a member of the CPD Certification Service. How to Become a Master of Persuasion is based on two accredited CPD training courses: Storytelling and Pitching an Idea.

CHAPTER 1

Why Persuasion Is at the Heart of Pitching

Being persuasive is an essential skill for everyone in business, especially those who work with customers or are involved in business development and sales.

Persuasion means inducing or leading someone to do something through reason and argument. Therefore, pitching is the process through which a supplier persuades a customer to buy its products, services, and solutions.

Customers are persuaded when they consider a supplier to meet their needs. How they arrive at this conclusion is not a matter of luck. Even having the best products does not guarantee winning. What determines success and failure is how well the supplier presents themselves.

This is determined by how well they align their business goals to those of the customer; how well they present their team, the company, and their products and services to the customer; how well they explain the benefits of choosing them versus a competitor; and how effectively they communicate all of this at numerous meetings with their customer throughout the sales process.

Sales Is a Process

Business is doomed unless it has a regular stream of sales. Sales are the life blood of business. They are the oxygen that a business needs to breathe.

The sales process is very much like a road trip. The end destination is known. However, the exact route is worked out along the way, and the route isn't in a supplier's hands because it is chosen by the customer. They decide the direction, which way to turn, the speed, and how long it will take.

The sales process can also be convoluted and its dynamics, and the activities that occur throughout it, are driven by a number of factors. Some may be unique to a particular industry, or to specific products and services, or to the circumstances and business needs driving a customer at that time.

Various models describe the business development process, and most of them picture it as a funnel with a number of steps. The idea is that the supplier travels along the funnel through these steps in turn, each step bringing them closer to the end point of winning.

Such models are useful in as much as they help a supplier's management team to estimate the value of potential sales in the pipeline and can provide a rough sense of where a specific customer is in the sales process. However, neither buyers nor customers view themselves as being at stages of these funnels in the same way suppliers might.

The models over simplify what is happening because they imagine the customer is traveling along the process in an orderly way, when in reality the sales process, like the car journey, is all over the place. Things move forward, but they can sometimes also stop, backtrack, and go around and around in circles.

This isn't because the customer is behaving in a maverick way. It is because evaluating suppliers isn't straightforward, and just as the supplier gains knowledge about what the customer wants over time, the customer also goes through a learning curve. The more the customer talks to potential suppliers and consults with internal colleagues and external advisers, the more it understands what it wants.

The second problem is that the funnel idea imagines the customer as though it were one entity, as though it has one mind. The job for the supplier is to move this mind along the funnel, as best it can.

Back in the real world, the customer is neither one entity nor one mind. There are usually several stakeholders who decide which supplier to select. Each stakeholder will have their own perspective and may also be in a completely different place in terms of decision making to their colleagues.

Therefore, from the beginning to the end of the sales process, the supplier needs to be alive to two things. The first is to expect that the journey will rarely be smooth and straightforward, or for that matter fast. Second, the customer sets the bar the supplier has to jump over to win, and since the customer comprises a number of individuals, to win, the supplier will have to convince all the stakeholders to choose them.

It is easy to think it is obvious what needs to be done to win. After all, isn't it simple? All a supplier has to do is to persuade the customer they have the best solution or products? But what does that mean? What it means is that the customer is persuaded to think the supplier has the right answers, the right products, the right people, and the right skills. They come to think a specific supplier meets their needs better than anyone else.

Customers are not persuaded by chance. Sometimes the process can happen quickly, because the customer has an urgent need and is in a hurry to make a decision. Normally, however, it takes time and effort for the supplier to persuade a customer to buy from them and happens as a result of their relationship deepening and developing as they get to know each other.

However long it takes, the supplier will interact with the customer several times, at face-to-face meetings, via documents and proposals, on phone calls, via e-mails and video conference calls, or via an e-procurement system.

Not all the meeting occasions are big moments in the sales process. Some are small steps. Each moment is important, because the customer evaluates everything a supplier says each time they are in touch. They look through a lens that is shaped by their understanding of their business needs, and sometimes also by their personal goals, and analyze and judge everything the supplier tells them.

It is sometimes said that first impressions count, and of course they do. However, so do second and third impressions. *The point is that every moment counts.* Every time a supplier interacts with a prospective customer, they have an opportunity to pitch their products and services, to reinforce key messages, and to persuade the customer that they are the right supplier to choose.

This is why success is in the hands of the supplier to quite a large extent, but only if everyone who represents the supplier, and who communicates with the customer, recognizes the importance of every meeting occasion and does everything they can to turn it to their advantage.

Communication Is at the Heart of Persuasion

Customers are persuaded when they come to believe a supplier's offer is better for them than anything being proposed by anyone else. However, persuasion isn't a gift that someone can be given. It can't be taken, like a magic potion. It's not a clever gimmick or a form of words that somehow guarantees success.

Persuasion is a state of mind brought about by how well the supplier pitches what it has to offer and communicates compelling reasons and arguments for being chosen.

A great sales pitch will therefore be interesting, engaging, informed, relevant, and compelling. It will answer the customer's key questions and concerns. It will show the customer how the supplier meets or exceeds their requirements and broader business objectives. It will set out why a supplier believes they have the best solution, as well as how they will deliver outstanding service and performance to the customer, in terms of products, processes, people, technology, expertise, and commitment.

This package of great things will be clearly so persuasive that the customer completely understands the benefits and compelling reasons for choosing a particular supplier.

Who wouldn't want their pitches to be this powerful and persuasive? The short answer is no one. However, this is not a formula for delivering a great pitch. Knowing that something is good is helpful but what counts is knowing how to do it.

The Formula of Persuasion

A simple formula for being persuasive is given as follows:

PROPOSITION × POSITIONING = PERSUASION.

The Proposition comes from the supplier having a clear understanding of the customer's business needs and their specific requirements, set against (or divided by) an honest and detailed appraisal of whether, and to what extent, they are able to deliver what the customer needs and wants.

The Positioning is how the proposition is turned into communication, which requires the supplier to identify compelling reasons, arguments, and justifications as to why the customer should buy from them, and the creation and delivery of documents, proposals, and presentations that speak to the customer in a way that is compelling and convincing.

The Persuasion[2] represents the number of opportunities that occur throughout the sales process when the supplier communicates with the customer and, therefore, has the opportunity to convince them that they are the right supplier to choose.

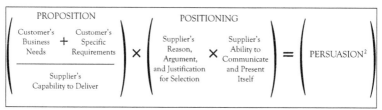

Figure 1.1 *The formula of persuasion*

Learning the Process of Persuasion

Persuasion doesn't happen by chance. Because being persuasive is the result of the supplier's capability to deliver what the customer needs and requires multiplied by how well they position themselves (the strength of the reasons and arguments for choosing them multiplied by their ability to communicate them), it becomes possible to see how the supplier can take a number of steps to persuade the customer.

These steps are a process the supplier can follow that will enhance their chances of success. The great thing about this is that a process can be learned and applied by any business to enable them to become a master of persuasion.

The process has a number of steps: the analysis of the customer's needs and requirements, the identification of what the supplier can offer the customer, working out the compelling reasons that explain why what the supplier is proposing is the best solution for the customer, producing documentation and presentations, and then engaging the customer at meetings, all of which are required in order to persuade a customer to choose the supplier.

This is what this entire book is about, teaching businesses how, if they can learn and apply this process, they can master the art of persuasion.

The process itself has three core activities—strategy, story, and delivery, which are divided into six steps, which are given as follows:

1. Communication Objective
2. Meeting Goal
3. Story Plan
4. Content
5. Style and Language
6. Pitch and Presentation

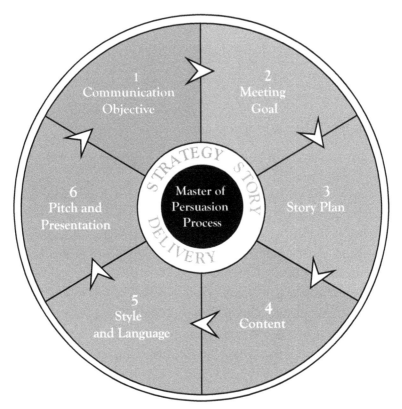

Figure 1.2 The process of persuasion

Step 1. Communication Objective

The Communication Objective explains how the supplier will position their proposal, describe key benefits, and convince the customer they are the best supplier to choose. This is driven by having a detailed understanding of what is happening in the customer's world, and therefore, what is driving business decision making, and being clear how they will meet or exceed the requirements set out by the customer.

Step 2. Meeting Goal

Throughout the sales process, there are numerous interactions between a supplier and a customer, and each one is an opportunity to pitch. The onus is on the supplier to work out how to handle each situation and to turn it to their advantage, taking into account the nature of the interaction, how their relationship with the customer has evolved so far, and what needs to happen next to push the relationship further along the sales process. This step explains how to do this.

Step 3. Story Plan

The Story Plan explains how to structure a script, document, or presentation, so themes and ideas are consistent, joined up, and comprehensible, therefore making it easier to understand, more engaging, and more interesting.

Step 4. Content

Businesses are run by people, who are both rational and emotional thinkers. In this step, suppliers learn how to profile customers, so they are able to choose content that both appeals to rational thinkers and addresses the issues and concerns of emotional thinkers.

Also, given there is always more content available than time to present it, it is important to select content that clearly and most powerfully communicates key messages.

Step 5. Style and Language

Words are the meaningful elements of speech and writing. Style is the way language is used. The combination of the words and the way they are used bring a Story Plan and Content to life, and ultimately persuades the customer to buy from a supplier.

Chapter 7 teaches how to develop a style and language that is assertive, evocative, explicit, and persuasive.

Step 6. Pitch and Presentation

Delivering a presentation is clearly the moment everything comes together, when content is heard, and the presenter or presentation team performs. This chapter teaches the presenter how to master their voice and physical presence to engage and enthrall an audience.

Each step in the process is explained in detail in separate chapters, and at the end of the book, there is a guide that explains how to use the process to transform an entire approach. The next chapter covers the foundation of persuasion, which is how to write a Communication Objective.

CHAPTER 2

Step 1—Communication Objective

A customer ultimately selects a supplier because they judge them to be the best one, when the purchasing decision is ultimately made. Customers are persuaded through rational argument, which means they have good reasons for choosing one supplier over another and are also able to justify why they've made this decision.

The decision-making process itself is usually far from simple, and there will be a number of reasons why they make a decision. The supplier will obviously be credible and able to meet requirements that have been detailed in documents and described at meetings. The customer may feel a supplier shares a similar culture to them. They may be thinking longer term and believe they will be able to build a deeper and more effective partnership with a particular supplier. They may value the skills and capabilities of one supplier more highly than another. Pricing will obviously have played an important part in the decision, although that does not necessarily mean the supplier who is the cheapest will always win.

Whatever the reasons, it is important to remember that the judgment or decision comes at the end of the sales process. Throughout the process, the customer's thinking has been shaped by the numerous discussions, proposals, presentations, and pitches they have had with a number of suppliers, as well as from the discussions that have happened internally, and with their advisers.

Therefore, the better the communication from the supplier, in terms of quality and impact, the more likely it is to persuade the customer. The more supplier is able to control what it communicates to the customer, the more likely it is to influence what they are thinking. This is why the entire process, and Communication Objective specifically, is so important in putting the supplier in the best position to win.

Communication Objective—Thinking

Every moment the supplier's pitch team interacts with the customer makes a difference and shapes their thinking. Ultimately, this leads the customer to the point where they believe they have identified the right supplier for them.

In practical terms, what has shaped the customer's thinking is what the supplier has communicated to them. How they have described and positioned their solution, products, and services, and how closely what they have put forward matches what the customer believes they want.

This is the sales process, that starts, in earnest, the moment the supplier identifies a genuine business opportunity, perhaps because they have spoken directly to the customer or they been invited to participate in a tender process.

At the outset, the supplier needs to understand what the customer wants and then to work out a strategy that will ultimately persuade the customer they have the best and most compelling solution.

This requires a detailed understanding of the customer's requirement, as well as their broader business needs, and for the supplier to assess their own capabilities as to how they will deliver everything the customer wants in full; and this needs to happen quickly, so that the supplier's pitch team understands how to talk to and communicate with the customer, from day 1.

The purpose of the Communication Objective, which is the first step in the process of becoming a Master of Persuasion, is to explain how the supplier will position their proposal, describe key benefits, and convince the customer through reason and argument that they are the best. The supplier, therefore, needs to understand the customer as deeply as possible, and this is achieved through Customer Profiling.

Customer Profiling is a methodology to probe a customer's business, to find out what is shaping their thinking and driving their decision making. The methodology has two inputs, Change Drivers and Customer Requirements.

1. Change Drivers assess what is driving the customer's business in terms of market conditions, ambition, regulation, and performance, that is, what is happening to the customer in their world.

2. Customer Requirements analysis is performed as to what the customer says they want to buy.

The process of analyzing Change Drivers and Customer Requirements should direct the supplier's entire approach to developing a winning solution. It should also drive communication, because the analysis highlights what matters most to the customer and therefore should be the focus of what the supplier talks to them about.

Change Drivers

The first input to profiling the customer is Change Drivers. Although requirements may be detailed, they do not exist in a bubble and are inevitably linked to what is happening to the customer's business. Therefore, understanding what the customer wants to buy in a wider context is both useful and insightful.

For example, why is the customer taking this approach, and why do they want to buy now? What business challenges is the customer facing, or will face in the medium or longer term? Are there any other factors that might be influencing the customer's business that could affect their choice of supplier or influence how they will make decisions?

There are four Change Drivers that will affect a customer's business strategically and operationally. They are market, ambition, performance, and regulation, and they are explained in detail in the following subsections.

Market

The market or sector a customer operates in will affect its current performance and influence its future business ambitions. There are two key questions the supplier should consider.

1. What are the challenges and opportunities facing the sector the customer operates in, in the short, medium, and longer term?
2. What should the supplier take into account when proposing their solution to the customer in the light of this information?

Understanding this enables the supplier to tailor what they propose to the customer after taking market conditions into account. For example, a supplier might be able to help the customer take steps to mitigate the negative consequences of changes in the market or conversely help them take advantage of new market opportunities.

A deeper understanding of the market challenges facing the customer enables the supplier to differentiate themselves from competitors. The supplier, armed with this knowledge, will be able to add value to and contribute more effectively to the future success of the customer than a supplier who does not understand the market the customer is operating in.

Ambition

For the same reason as understanding market conditions is important, knowing the business strategy of the customer can help the supplier identify the best solution to propose. Imagine, for example, how the supplier would change their approach if they knew the customer intended to expand the number of territories they operate in, to contract or diversify their business interests or have acquired or sold parts of their existing businesses in recent times?

A customer's future business strategy may also create additional business opportunities for a supplier. For example, it may be relevant for the supplier to make the customer aware of its wider capabilities, in addition to those that are pertinent to winning the specific tender or contract under consideration now, because they can see how their capabilities will be relevant in the future.

Customers often set out their ambitions on their website, in annual reports, and in other public and Internet spaces. If they are a listed company, they are required to provide shareholders and investors with details about their plans and intentions, as well as financial reports, compliance, and business and operational structure.

Another pressing thing to find out is why the customer wants to change their current supplier? What is driving the decision to look elsewhere, and how should understanding this desire to change be taken into account by the supplier?

Performance

The financial performance of a business is also instructive. A number of indicators tell their own story regarding the current financial health of a company, including gross and net profit, working capital and current ratio, and so on.

Understanding the current health of a potential customer, from a financial perspective, may explain why they have listed certain specifications and requirements or point to the criteria that may be used to assess supplier proposals.

Underpinning a business relationship is a commercial relationship. Therefore, understanding a customer's financial position may inform the commercial negotiation, including payment structure, risk mitigation, pricing, payment, and other terms.

Regulation

What is meant by regulation are the laws and mandatory rules, set by governments and regulatory bodies, which customers are required to comply with. Of course, regulation doesn't apply to every customer. It depends on what they do. However, when it does, it has a significant impact on a customer's business, in terms of day-to-day operations, business structure, processes, and reporting.

Understanding what regulations are changing is also extremely useful, not least because changes are usually set out well in advance. Therefore, it should be possible to find out how new rules will affect the way a business operates, which means the supplier should know how these will affect their relationship with the customer, what might change in order to comply with new rules, and how they can help the customer deal with the impact of new regulation or legislation in the future.

Change Driver Analysis

The purpose of analyzing Change Drivers is to understand what is happening in the customer's world. However, this is not intended to be an activity which is performed for its own sake. The purpose for the supplier is to

			PERFORMANCE	ANALYSIS
MARKET	Strength	Weakness		
	Opportunity	Threat		
REGULATION	Strength	Weakness	AMBITION	
	Opportunity	Threat		

Figure 2.1 Customer profile change drivers worksheet

find out what will help them to build a better relationship with the customer, and to understand whether the customer is planning or responding
to changes that will have a far reaching or material impact on the supplier's
ability to deliver what the customer requires from them in future.

The Customer Profile Change Drivers Worksheet (Figure 2.1) can be
used to detail key findings.

Market and Regulation are SWOT diagrams that should be completed as though from the supplier's perspective. For example, a "market
strength" will be something that is an advantage to the supplier, whereas
a "regulatory threat" would be a challenge.

The Performance square should contain the key financial metrics
about the customer and include any concerns that are relevant to working
for them in the future or need to be considered in terms of the commercial proposal.

The Ambition square should detail known customer business
objectives and include notes explaining in what way they are relevant to
helping the supplier win the current business opportunity.

Analysis is the place to highlight points that need to be taken into
account by the pitch team as they put together the solution they will

Personal Insight

Working as a consultant with some of the biggest companies, it always surprised me how little they knew about the customers they were pitching to. They knew the customer's brand, of course, and a fair amount about their business. However, they didn't routinely do any meaningful research. What they knew amounted to general information, and certainly nothing that would help them win a contract. This lack of real in-depth knowledge came home to me on one I occasion I remember really well. I'd been invited to join a pitch team, for a client I'd never worked with before. As the new-bie and a paid consultant, I could tell the pitch team weren't that pleased to see me at the meeting. The meeting was to brainstorm the approach my client was going to take, and after a fairly meaningless 30 minutes of chit-chat, one of the senior managers turned to me and asked, "Since you're the consultant. What do you think we should do?" I'd done a little research, and in the customer's annual report found out, they had acquired four companies in the previous 12 months, and the Chairman and CEO both explained why they were diversifying the business and their plans to expand further in the coming two years. So, I asked the team whether they thought the decision to put out legal immigration and support servicers out to tender (which is what my client does) was linked to the customer's expansion plans? "What expansion plans?" was their response. An hour later, we had mapped customers current footprint to a world map, and also mapped where my client was based. Then, we looked at the gaps and speculated where the customer might buy next, and how my client would service their requirement as their business grew. Secondly, we debated why the tender had been issued now, and in a way, with a little thought, it became obvious. The customer's current advisers were American based only, and therefore had been outgrown. The conversation changed the entire direction of focus, so that from that moment my client became focused not only on proposing the delivery of a great service but also on positioning themselves in terms of their international credentials and how they would build their services out as and when the customer acquired new companies in new territories.

propose to the customer. These may also be points for discussion and should also influence future communication with the customer.

Customer Requirements

The second input to profile a customer is to understand what the customer wants to buy. This is obtained by analyzing the documents they provide, through direct discussions with stakeholders, from what has been learnt about the customer's world and from relevant technology and business trends. All this information provides context and insight into the requirements the customer says they want to buy.

The analysis of requirements should, as a minimum, answer these six questions:

1. What does the customer want to achieve in terms of project goals and are they being realistic?
2. What specific products, solutions, and services does the customer require? Will these requirements deliver the customer's intended project goal and is the supplier able to meet these requirements in full?
3. Does the supplier think the customer has a full and complete understanding of what they need or are there gaps, contradictions or anomalies in what the customer has asked for?
4. Does the supplier believe there are better ways of achieving the customer's goals?
5. What deadlines has the customer requested, and will the supplier be able to meet them?
6. What resources will the supplier need, and will they be available?

It is important to assess requirements objectively, and in detail. It isn't unusual for customers to have a set of requirements that are extremely broad and extensive; to the point it would seem they have listed everything humanly possible. Of course, the more extensive the requirement, the more extensive and expensive the solution.

It is therefore important to work through the stated requirements to obtain a realistic assessment of what the priorities of the customer really are, and whether what they are asking actually makes sense and has been thought through properly.

The second aspect of this analysis is to enable the supplier to critique its own capabilities. Are they able to deliver everything the customer has asked for, or are there weaknesses and gaps in what they are able to provide or deliver?

Detailed analysis of the resources required to deliver what the customer wants is also important, and resource availability needs to be assessed at the outset. If there are any resource constraints, they need to be fully understood in order to plan how they will be dealt with.

Project timings and deadlines are also very important and should be considered before any proposal or solution is put forward by a supplier. It may be necessary to deploy additional resources to hit deadlines, if timings are aggressive. This may increase internal costs, change the project risk profile, and change the commercial proposal.

If what the customer is aiming to achieve isn't realistic or doesn't fit within standard practices deployed by the supplier, then identifying potential delivery issues from the start enables the pitch team to discuss them with the customer and provides both the time and the opportunity to resolve issues or shortcomings.

Anomalies are also very important and useful things to identify. Requirements that do not make sense or perhaps haven't been thought through enough, including any obvious gaps and contradictions, provide opportunities for the supplier to engage meaningfully with the customer, and add a lot of value in helping the customer to improve their approach, and to clearly differentiate themselves from the competition.

For example, a supplier may have delivered something similar to another customer before. They may, therefore, know how the customer's approach can be improved. They may well be able to demonstrate the benefits of their experience using a case study, which is extremely persuasive and provides the customer with good reasons for selecting a supplier.

The list of anomalies could become a future meeting agenda, and the insight this provides could also enable the supplier to differentiate themselves from competitors.

Having completed the analysis of requirements, the supplier's pitch team may well have written a number of notes, and this information needs to be brought together so it can be understood and used by every-one involved in the sales process, and one way of doing that is to use the Requirement Analysis Chart.

Requirement Analysis Chart

The Requirement Analysis Chart (Figure 2.2) shows the supplier's strengths and weaknesses in a visual way. The chart takes all the requirements listed by the customer and allows the supplier to plot them in terms of their ability and confidence to meet or deliver each requirement in full.

The chart separates requirements in terms of their importance to the customer versus the supplier's own analysis of their ability to deliver them.

Analysis Chart Quadrants

- Quadrant 1 shows requirements of high importance to the customer where the supplier's offering is strong.
- Quadrant 2 shows requirements of high importance to the customer where the supplier's offering is weak.
- Quadrant 3 shows requirements of low importance to the customer where the supplier's offering is strong.
- Quadrant 4 shows requirements of low importance to the customer where the supplier's offering is weak.

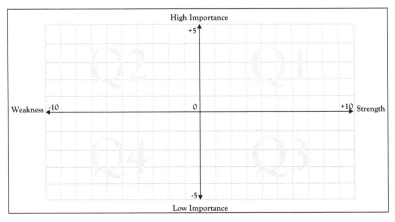

Figure 2.2 Requirement analysis chart

The visual representation of relative strengths and weaknesses provides two useful pieces of information. First, it is a clear visual representation of what is important to the customer, and second, it shows by comparison the self-assessed capabilities of the supplier (their strengths and weaknesses).

Everything that appears in Quadrant 2 is a major problem, and to a lesser extent, this also applies to Quadrant 4. Everything in Quadrants 1 and 3 show the requirements the supplier is confident they can deliver in full.

Requirements that are of high importance and high strength can be communicated confidently when talking to the customer.

The requirements that fall into Quadrants 2 and 4 are weaknesses according to the supplier's own self-assessment. The supplier needs to pass judgment as to how important the requirements in this are to their chances of winning. Those that are really important clearly need to be at the top of the supplier's to-do-list, as solving these deficiencies and gaps may well hold the key to winning future work and therefore cannot be ignored.

How to Write a Communication Objective

The Communication Objective brings everything learned from profiling together in one place. Its purpose is to help the supplier's pitch team to position their proposal, describe key benefits, and convince the customer, through reasons and argument, that they are the best supplier.

By profiling the customer, the supplier will have identified significant Change Drivers. Whether driven by the market, their ambition, financial performance, or regulation, the supplier needs to consider how this knowledge will be used when communicating with the customer, in documents, meetings, pitches, and presentations.

The analysis of Customer Requirements, and the ability of the supplier to deliver them, will have made clear what are the most important requirements and whether the supplier can deliver them in full. The features and benefits of how the supplier will meet the most important requirements of the customer need also to be communicated, if the customer is going to be persuaded to choose the supplier.

Therefore, the next step is to document what will be communicated, which is done by completing the Communication Objective Plan (COP).

Communication Objective Plan

The COP (Figure 2.3) brings the supplier's thinking together in one document that is a guide for everyone who will be communicating with the customer throughout the sales process.

The plan is separated into two parts. The first section is a list of significant Change Drivers. The second section is a list of the top Customer Requirements. Each section can have as many rows as is necessary to cover the points identified during profiling.

Change Drivers > Communication Strategy

The supplier adds a list of Change Drivers in order of importance, and under Communication Strategy sets out the key points that will be communicated, so it is clear to the customer both that the supplier understands what's happening in their world and how they have adapted their approach accordingly.

Top Customer Requirements > Benefits/Key Features to Communicate

Top Customer Requirements are listed in order of priority on the left-hand column, and the list of key features and benefits that will be communicated to the customer are added to the right-hand column.

COMMUNICATION OBJECTIVE PLAN	
Change Drivers	**Communication Strategy**
• List of change drivers in order of importance.	• Key points that will be communicated to the customer.
Top Customer Requirements	**Benefits/Key Features to Communicate**
• Top customer requirements in order in order of priority.	• Key features and benefits that will be communicated to the customer.

Figure 2.3 Communication objective plan template

Whenever communication is being created, ahead of every meeting, the supplier's pitch team should refer to the Communication Objective to make sure they are including these key messages and should also reinforce them when they speak to the customer, whenever possible.

Example Communication Objective—Positioning to Service the Customer's Current and Future Plans

How to complete a Communication Objective can be illustrated using a real example. This example shows how profiling can have a significant impact on the way a supplier positions themselves in terms of the customer's future plans.

The supplier, in this case study, is a global medical instrument manufacturer tendering to provide testing equipment and support services to a large pharmaceutical company with manufacturing sites in a number of countries in Europe (Figure 2.4).

The customer has issued a request for proposal (RFP) for a major contract and invited the supplier to put forward a proposal. One of the key requirements raised in the RFP was the importance of the supplier having a proven track record in delivering remote diagnostic services as part of a broad technical support package.

On researching the customer, the supplier came across a news story on a business news portal that reported the customer was in negotiation to buy an American competitor, which has manufacturing facilities in the United States as well as across Asia.

The RFP is focused only on purchasing equipment and services in Europe and has made no mention of the U.S. acquisition. However, since the supplier has offices in the United States and Asia, as well as Europe, it sees the potential of being able to fully service the customer in the new territories as well, should the acquisition go ahead. It is, therefore, important that the customer recognizes their full global capabilities.

In this example, the potential acquisition has been listed as a significant Change Driver. Therefore, in terms of Communication Strategy, the supplier has identified two actions. The first is to emphasize their European capabilities, so it is clear they are capable of meeting the customer's requirements in full.

COMMUNICATION OBJECTIVE PLAN CASE STUDY 1 – MEDICAL INSTRUMENT MANUFACTURER	
Change Drivers	**Communication Strategy**
• The customer is in negotiations to buy a company in the United States, with manufacturing capabilities in the United States and Asia, where the supplier also has offices. The customer may, therefore, need additional services in both new territories, in the near future.	• Focus on the supplier's capabilities to supply and support the customer's European and Asia plants immediately. • Show how the supplier will be able to quickly service new territories (including new plants in the United States and Asia) should the customer require them to. So as the customer's business grows, the supplier will be able to fully service their requirements.
Top Customer Requirements	**Benefits/Key Features to Communicate**
• High quality instruments.	• Meets all U.S. and European manufacturing standard. • Track record and history solely as a medical instrument manufacturer, with significant and proven Research and Development capabilities.
• Diagnostic support capabilities.	• Award-wining diagnostic tools are integral to the technology solution. • Automatic configurable alarm triggers support response. • Sophisticated fault diagnostic tools.
• In-country engineering and support services.	• Strong technical capabilities in country, with a proven track record. • On-site engineers work closely with Research and Development who also have access to top engineers.

Figure 2.4 Communication objective plan: case study 1—Medical instrument manufacturer

With an eye on the opportunity to service the customer in the United States and Asia, the supplier will also reference its global capabilities and how easy and straightforward it will be to expand their capabilities to other territories if and when required. The supplier wants the customer to hear and remember that their footprint is global, and as the customer's business grows, they are going to be able to scale the service they offer.

In terms of requirements, the supplier has listed the top three identified during profiling. Against each requirement are benefits and features that underline how the supplier will meet and exceed the customer's requirement. In the same way, the significant Change Drivers should be communicated to the customer, so should the benefits and features, listed in the worksheet.

In both cases, the worksheet makes clear what the supplier wants the customer to hear and remember in respect of their capabilities to meet their requirements now and in the future. These points, therefore, should be prominent in discussions, proposal documents, and presentations.

Summarizing the Communication Objective

The Communication Objective is the first step in the process of becoming a Master of Persuasion. It is focused on strategy because it is essential that the supplier, from the outset, understands what is important to the customer and what they want to achieve. This becomes a platform for communicating with the customer at every step of the sales process.

Winning work cannot be accomplished without a detailed understanding of the customer's business needs and requirements, which is achieved by profiling them. Profiling has two parts: understanding the customer's world through analyzing Change Drivers, and a detailed analysis of their requirements including an honest assessment of the supplier's capabilities to deliver everything the customer wants in full.

Some of this analysis may well inform aspects of the supplier's wider proposal strategy. However, the focus, in terms of communication, is to determine an effective and persuasive Communication Objective that provides direction and guidance to the supplier's pitch team in future discussions with the customer.

As the relationship between the supplier and customer develops, of course, the information gathered through Customer Profiling may well be updated and clarified, and this may, in turn, require the Communication Objective to be updated too, to reflect this new understanding.

The next two steps in the process, Meeting Goal and Story Plan, explain how to turn the Communication Objective into a powerful business story which provides the compelling reasons and arguments to persuade the customer to buy from a supplier.

CHAPTER 3

Step 2—Meeting Goal

Throughout the sales process, the customer and supplier will interact at various meetings. Whether a phone call, a video conference, or a face-to-face meeting, each occasion provides the supplier with the opportunity to persuade the customer they offer the best solution, and ultimately, they are the right supplier to choose.

A key part of what the supplier should talk about comes from the Communication Objective. It reveals what is happening in the customer's world, provides the broad themes the supplier should communicate to the customer, and identifies their priorities in terms of requirements.

Every meeting provides a unique opportunity to engage with and persuade the customer and should be prepared for thoroughly. This means having a specific plan of action as to how it should be approached, which is the purpose of the Meeting Goal.

The sales process is not in the control of a supplier. However, that does not mean the supplier doesn't influence what happens at a specific meeting. Therefore, the supplier, as well as having a very clear idea where they are in the sales process currently, should also have a clear opinion as to what can be achieved from this specific meeting to help them progress along the sale process. After all, from a business or professional perspective, if they are not focused, then they are wasting their and their employer's time and money.

Meeting Goal Thinking

Imagine the supplier's relationship with a customer has two states. The first is the current state, meaning where the relationship is now. The second is the future state, which is where the supplier wants the relationship to be in the future. What the supplier needs to focus on is how they are going to move the relationship closer to the future state at the next meeting they have planned with the customer.

The current state encompasses everything the customer knows about the supplier, including products, services, history, financial performance, business footprint, and so on.

Moving further along the sales process toward the future state is achieved by challenging customer perceptions and by enhancing the customer's understanding and appreciation of the supplier's capabilities, products, services, and solutions. The supplier should also consider their relationship, and whether the customer's attitude toward them is warm and positive, cool and negative, or even ambivalent.

It is always worth remembering that whatever shortcomings there may be, any aspect of a relationship between the customer and the supplier can be changed. Every problem can be overcome. The starting point to effect change is to realize what's missing or what's wrong and then to do something about it.

How to Write a Meeting Goal

To prepare for the meeting, the supplier should consider the following:

- How far have they progressed along the sales process? If progress has been slow, what has prevented the supplier from moving forward faster, and if there are obstacles or issues, what do they need to do to overcome them?
- Since the sales process commenced, what have they learned about the customer that challenges their original understanding? Does this new knowledge change the Communication Objective?
- Does the customer fully appreciate the extent of the supplier's capabilities to meet the customer's requirement, and if not, what capabilities need to be highlighted or discussed in greater detail?
- Do they think they are serious contenders to win the contract or be appointed? If not, what is holding the supplier back and how can it change the relationship with the customer in its favor?
- If the customer has an agenda for the meeting, what is driving their choice of topics? Do they indicate the customer has

concerns in terms of what the supplier is proposing that need to be discussed (and therefore prepared for in ahead of the meeting)?

- What doesn't the customer know about the supplier? What relevant information will enhance the customer's opinion of them?

Meeting Goal

Having thought through the current and future state of the relationship, the next step is for the supplier to set their thinking down in writing, using the Meeting Goal worksheet (Figure 3.1).

Gaps in a Customer's Knowledge

The starting point is to identify gaps in the Customer's Knowledge. What doesn't the customer know about the supplier that is relevant to shaping their thinking and, secondly, what will move the relationship from the current to the future state?

The supplier should be thinking about whether they have been able to communicate the points they identified in the Communication Objective. Whether the customer properly understands what the supplier has to offer and appreciates their capabilities? Whether the customer understands how the supplier's products work, how they are made, and what distinguishes them from other suppliers?

It stands to reason that if a customer after meeting the supplier does not learn anything new about them, then the relationship will have gone backward. For the customer to gain a deeper understanding requires the

MEETING GOAL WORKSHEET TEMPLATE	
Gaps in a Customer's Knowledge	**Perceptions to Challenge**
• What doesn't the customer know about the supplier that is relevant?	• In what way does the customer not perceive them correctly?
Topics for Discussion	**Positioning**
• What topics should the supplier discuss with the customer that will provide a structure to the meeting?	• How will the supplier introduce and explain this topic to the customer?

Figure 3.1 Meeting Goal worksheet template

supplier to tell them something new, and to not only inform the customer of something but also explain why it is relevant to them and why they need to know.

Perceptions to Challenge

The customer's perceptions of the supplier are important and influence the final choice they will make, and if the supplier thinks the customer does not perceive them correctly, then they will need to do something about it.

Of course, what a customer really thinks of a supplier and how they regard their capabilities are not simple or easy things to detect.

However, the supplier may pick up a subtle nuance in conversation with the customer that leads them to think there is an issue, problem, or a concern they need to address. Other indicators that the customer may have a negative perception of the supplier can be found in the questions they ask, or the agenda points they set ahead of a meeting. However, it is important the supplier doesn't jump to assumptions about what the questions mean too quickly, without thinking carefully first.

One obvious example of a customer who has concerns is one who seeks reassurance about a product's performance or questions the nature of the support they will receive or whether the supplier's team has the skills and expertise the customer requires. These questions indicate a genuine a concern. Addressing such concerns can be straightforward and can be tackled head on. However, sometimes it isn't easy to shift the customer's doubts. This, therefore, may be something the supplier needs to keep working on at future meetings; and clearly, this is something that will need to be carefully planned.

Topics for Discussion

Having identified gaps and perceptions that need to be challenged, the supplier should next set out the topics they want to discuss with the customer that will provide a structure to the meeting so the relationship can move on. The point is that if the supplier is going to tackle an issue (for their benefit), it needs to be on their agenda in the first place!

Positioning

Positioning is how the supplier will introduce and explain this topic to the customer. It is the context as to why the supplier thinks a particular issue is worth discussing or covering in a presentation. Context is really important because it sets the scene, and it moves the mind of the customer into the right place to start listening to what the supplier is trying to explain.

Example Meeting Goal—Changing the Delivery Strategy

The approach to writing a Meeting Goal can be illustrated using a real example. This example is taken from the Meeting Goal of the second case study in Chapter 5, which is titled "Changing the Delivery Strategy."

The company (supplier) provides implant office support services to major corporations, which requires them to put staff on the ground in the offices of their customers to deliver a number of back-office services (Figure 3.2). The supplier was asked to respond to a tender document which, as normal, detailed the requirements of the customer. Since then, they have had a number of face-to-face meetings which led them initially to recommend a solution and outline a transition plan.

The supplier now realizes their assumptions at the outset have led them to propose an unworkable solution to the customer and they now need to change their entire approach if they are to be successful moving forward. The question is how should they present this to the customer positively?

The gap in the Customer's Knowledge explains why the supplier jumped to the wrong conclusions. The assumption reached from the outset was that the way the supplier's services would operate would be the same for every department. However, it turns out that each department works in a fundamentally different way to others. This is the gap in the customer's thinking that the supplier needs to fill.

Both the customer and the supplier had based their thinking on the supplier's previous experience working with other customers. This was

MEETING GOAL	
CASE STUDY 2 – IMPLANT OFFICE SUPPORT SERVICES COMPANY	
Gaps in a Customer's Knowledge	**Perceptions to Challenge**
• The customer's original approach was to roll out implant services throughout the company in one go. What they haven't taken into account is the level of customization that will be necessary to ensure services work effectively in each department.	• The supplier's response to the customer's brief was based on previous solutions they provided to other customers. This was a mistake. Now it is clear the proposed approach will not work, the supplier needs to bring customer with them in changing their approach, without losing credibility.
Topics for Discussion	**Positioning**
• Problems with current approach. • The revised project plans. • Benefits of the new plan in terms of risks, resources, and costs.	• The supplier has identified a better approach than originally proposed, which has a number of significant benefits. • Changing the approach will lead to much more effective and tailored implementation plans for each department.

Figure 3.2 Meeting Goal: case study 2—implant office support services company

clearly the root of the mistake. Therefore, the perception the supplier needs to challenge is that the one-size-fits-all approach is a viable one, when in fact the approach needs to be customized to the detailed and specific requirements of each department, if it is to work effectively.

The list of Topics for Discussion flows from the gaps and challenges. What's wrong with the current approach needs to be discussed in detail, so the customer understands what the problem is. The alternative approach, now being proposed by the supplier, also needs to be explained. These changes will affect the rollout plan, the resources required to deliver the plan, and the costs of the project moving forward, and therefore, they also need to be discussed in detail. Finally, there is good news because the revised approach will deliver a number of benefits, each of which also needs to be explained.

Positioning is also important. The difficulty for the supplier is that the plan was their suggestion, not the customer's. Therefore, this whole situation is an embarrassment to the supplier. However, a much more positive approach to the meeting is to position the changes required as being the result of the supplier identifying a better way of doing things, which has a number of significant benefits for the customer in terms of effectiveness, costs, and long-term value.

Summarizing the Meeting Goal

The themes that have been identified in the Communication Objective are relevant at every step of the sales process. The Meeting Goal is how the supplier focuses on preparing for a specific meeting with the customer, for the express purpose of moving their relationship further along the sales process, by taking it from the current to the future state.

The Meeting Goal provides a clear direction for the supplier and enables them to write the business story that will become the substance of a presentation that will be delivered to the customer or the agenda for discussion when they next meet the customer.

The next step in the process, Story Plan, is where the detail is added, and how this step in the process works is explained in the next chapter.

Personal Insight

Who goes to a meeting with a prospective customer without doing any preparation? Well, the answer, if you ask me, is a lot of qualified and highly trained professional people! In fact, for many people, the modus operandi is to wing it. To think on one's feet and almost to take a degree of pride in handling things this way. As a consultant, it actually is relatively easy to show why this is not the best approach. I joined a meeting with a client's pitch team, once, to discuss a new business opportunity. The VP, who will be leading the pitch, was delayed, so the meeting, which was also attended by the CEO of my client, started without them. The focus for the pitch team was the requirement document that had been issued by the customer. So, the team went through it in detail and made a list of everything that was either incomplete or wasn't clear, so these points could be taken up with the customer. All this happened before the VP finally arrives, and when they do, they are full of themselves. They've had a great meeting with the customer, and they are fired up, and very enthusiastic, that is until the CEO puts the questions to them. Does he know the answer to any of these questions? The answer is no. The meeting the VP has just had, covered things in general. In fact, they have learned nothing new. So, another meeting has to be planned, if the customer agrees, and the message to the team and the VP from the CEO is a simple one. Don't waste your time and my money again.

CHAPTER 4

Step 3—Story Plan

Describing business communication as being like a story might seem fanciful. Everyone knows that a book or a film or a TV show has been planned in advance and has a script or story as well as a structure. Can a discussion, a business presentation, or a proposal document be compared to a story?

One thing that is similar is the intended end result. Whether a film, a novel, or a thought-provoking business presentation, they all share the same purpose, which is to engage an audience.

There is no reason why business communication cannot be engaging, interesting, educational, provocative, or even enjoyable in its own way. The question, therefore, is how do businesses engage their audience? How do they enhance their ability to write a thought-provoking or enjoyable presentation or tell a more effective and persuasive business story? More importantly, in terms of the sales process, how does a supplier construct a story that not only engages but also convinces and persuades a customer to buy from them?

Few people, who have worked in business for any length of time, haven't suffered the experience of sitting through a presentation that didn't work: One that didn't communicate anything interesting or one that didn't add value. This isn't about superficial likes and dislikes. Something we all share is the ability to recognize when something is done well, and something is done well when it has been thought through and made relevant to the audience that are listening to it or reading it.

To do something well, therefore, requires effort, and the result of putting in effort will be a story that is more engaging, more relevant, more effective, and more persuasive, and one that achieves its business purpose, its Meeting Goal.

Story Plan Thinking

There are many different approaches to writing a story. For example, approaches to writing a novel can be classified as parallel (having multiple storylines), linear and chronological, nonlinear and fragmented, and circular. The approaches to writing a speech are often described as categorical, biographical, causal, and comparative.

The question, therefore, is how do people in business take these different approaches on board, and can they be used to enhance a business story, so it is more effective and persuasive, and therefore worth the effort of trying?

Unlike the script, the business story is told, to some extent, on numerous occasions. It is re-enacted as a meeting agenda, a presentation, or a proposal document. Therefore, the story needs to be reshaped or tailored to fit the occasion the supplier will be in front of the customer.

Tailoring the story, however, does not actually make it harder or more complex to write. In fact, the task is made easier and more straightforward because what drives each enaction is the Communication Objective and the Meeting Goal. These set out the key themes that should be referred to, a list of topics to discuss for good reasons, and how they should be positioned at the meeting in respect of the customer.

Therefore, the task of writing a business story is not one of inventing a clever or gripping narrative, but it is about assembling a Story Plan that covers the themes, topics, and specific details that have already been agreed upon. These are the things the supplier needs to talk to the customer about, in a way that will be engaging and logical, that will make sense to the audience, reading or listening to it.

How to Write a Story Plan

To assemble the business story is best described as a sorting process, which requires the supplier to determine the sequence of the topics that will be in the document, agenda, pitch, or presentation they are preparing.

What should determine the Topic Running Order are the priorities from the supplier's perspective, as to what topics are more important than others and which themes connect the topics together.

For a business story to be effective, the themes that run throughout it must be both joined up and comprehensible. From an audience perspective, this is what makes a business story easier to follow, and if it is not easy to follow, it will neither be engaging nor enjoyable.

Being joined up means there are reasons or a logic for topics to flow in a particular sequence. What informs key reasons is the positioning set out in the Meeting Goal. Remember, positioning means finding a reason to explain the relevance or context of the topic from the customer's perspective. Therefore, the supplier needs not only to prioritize topics but also to think about the context from the customer's point of view. What will make most sense to them?

Story Plan Worksheet

The Story Plan Worksheet (Figure 4.1) is a simple layout, in three parts, that helps to structure a business story. The first column contains the Topic Running Order, taken from the Meeting Goal, explained in the previous chapter.

The second column on the right-hand side details the specific content or points that will be covered. The third and final part is Key Messages, where the supplier sets out important messages that they want the customer to hear and to remember.

STORY PLAN WORKSHEET	
Topic Running Order	**Content List**
• List topics in the order or sections that make sense, and ensure the points that are covered belong together and there is a rationale for the sequence.	• A detailed list of points that will be covered under each topic.
Key Messages	
• A list of the positive and persuasive things the supplier wants the customer to hear and remember .	

Figure 4.1 Story plan worksheet template

Topic Running Order

It is worth remembering when putting together a running order that good stories don't jump about from topic to topic randomly. In novel writing or script writing terms, this approach is known as a nonlinear or fragmented story, where events or sequences do not happen logically or chronologically. Used to structure a business story, this approach will be extremely confusing to the audience.

Instead, a good business story leads the audience to a new understanding or insight through a series of topics that seem to flow seamlessly from one to the next in a logical way and for understandable reasons.

This does not mean the story cannot have a number of sections, each one covering a different topic. It simply means that the order or sections make sense, and the points that are covered in each section belong together and there is a rationale for the sequence in which they will be covered.

Content List

The Content List should only be completed once the Topic Running Order has been written and agreed. This is a detailed list of points that will be covered under each topic. Point A should be taken from the Topic Running Order, and then the detailed list of points needs to be added underneath.

Just as with the list of topics, the flow of the detailed list of points is just as important. It also needs be logical and flow smoothly. As well as adding the detail, the supplier also needs to start to think about the number of pages or timings (if a presentation) it will take to properly cover each point. Clearly, there will always be constraints, and therefore every Story Plan should be realistic.

Key Messages

Key Messages come from the positioning identified in the Meeting Goal. These messages are the positive and persuasive things the supplier wants the customer to hear and remember (also known as takeaways). The purpose of a key message, from a communication perspective, is to draw attention to and underline positive messages about the supplier, their products, services, and solutions.

The idea that there should be certain qualities the supplier wants the customer to understand about themselves is not a new idea. The problem is that many messages (and qualities) are often stated subliminally. The supplier builds the case for a key message in a document or presentation that in their own mind is clear and obvious. However, it is left to the customer to recognize all the parts and to put them together, to get the message.

One of the golden rules of pitching is to make things as easy as possible for the customer. Therefore, it is impractical and also quite risky to expect a customer to put in a lot of effort to work out what a supplier is trying to communicate. Risky because if hidden subliminally then it is just as likely the customer will come to a completely different conclusion to the one the supplier intended.

It is best practice, therefore, to ensure that key messages are communicated directly to the customer. They can be in the introductory and closing paragraphs of a proposal or the opening and closing statements of a presentation. The important point is to make sure key messages are communicated.

Including key messages in the Story Plan Worksheet serves two purposes. The first is to make sure everyone in the supplier's pitch team know what they are, and second is to test whether the proposed structure (of topics and content) match the key messages the supplier intended to communicate.

If the structure of the Story Plan does not enable the team to communicate key messages, then either the messages were wrong in the first place, or the Story Plan, as it stands, needs to be adjusted.

Why Using a Previous Presentation Be a Mistake?

There is nothing wrong with reusing content from a previous presentation. However, the structure and content of an old presentation should not be the starting point when creating a new presentation because it is likely to create a lot of extra editing later on.

Previous presentations will have been written and presented to an entirely different customer. They will tell a different story to the one that is needed now for this new potential customer, and the key messages are likely be different too.

Instead, it is much better to work out a Story Plan for each new situation driven by a specific Communication Objective and Meeting Goal, written solely with the new customer in mind. Using previously created content is sensible, but only once the story is clear.

Why a Presentation Structure Should Be Driven by the Story

Structuring a presentation into sections so that it accommodates a list of speakers is also a common mistake, and one that is unlikely to produce the most persuasive presentation. Fundamentally, this approach prioritizes seniority or role over coherence and impact.

Of course, having sections in a story is perfectly fine and there is nothing wrong with having multiple speakers at a presentation either. What is paramount, however, is that the content addresses the issues, gaps, and questions that need to be covered and for the story to flow smoothly from beginning to end, so that it is easy to follow and it asserts the arguments and reasons that are most persuasive.

Starting with a blank sheet of paper can seem daunting. However, it is much better to set out intentions based on detailed thinking than to grab a previous presentation or to structure a presentation based on the speakers who are supposed to be presenting.

Example Story Plan—Changing the Delivery Strategy

This example details the next step in preparing a presentation to a customer that was described in the previous chapter. The supplier has proposed an unworkable solution and now needs to change their entire approach.

The Meeting Goal set out the gaps in the Customer's Knowledge, the Perceptions to Challenge, the Topics for Discussion (shown in the following section), and the Positioning. The next step in the process is for the supplier to write the Story Plan to deliver the goal they have set themselves.

Topics for Discussion

- Problems with current approach
- The revised project plans
- Benefits of the new plan in terms of risks, resources, and costs

The list of Topics for Discussion sets a clear agenda. Having realized the original approach is flawed, the reasons why it won't work need to be disclosed. The supplier has come up with an alternative plan which will affect approach, timings, resources, and cost; all of which also need to be discussed in detail.

Reference to the Positioning is also very relevant. The difficulty facing the supplier is that the plan was their suggestion, not the customers. Therefore, this whole situation is an embarrassment to the supplier. However, this new approach is being positioned positively. The new approach offers significant benefits for the customer in almost every respect.

The next step for the supplier's pitch team is to take the ideas from the Meeting Goal into writing the Story Plan, which sets out their approach in detail.

Topic Running Order

Topic Running Order is the structure of the presentation and the likely titles for each section in the order they will be discussed. The first topic, "What is wrong with the current approach?," is the starting point of the

STORY PLAN WORKSHEET	
CASE STUDY 2 - IMPLANT OFFICE SUPPORT SERVICES COMPANY	
Topic Running Order	**Content List**
• What is wrong with the current approach? • Proposed new approach in detail. • Key benefits of the new approach. • Next steps.	What is wrong with the current approach? • Explain Current Approach. • Go through the analysis of the current approach in terms of risk profile, the challenges of resourcing the project currently, and how the approach makes it difficult to meet the needs of every department. • Summarize issues and problems. Proposed new approach • Proposed approach to pilot one department and apply learnings in a phased roll-out. • Timing and delivery plan. • How this will change project staging costs.
Key Messages	
• The supplier's primary concern is to ensure the project is successful. They could keep going, but this is not in the customer's best long-term interests. • For this to be the start of a meaningful partnership the supplier needs to be truthful and tell the customer what they really think. • There are a number of benefits to the approach the supplier is now proposing, and fewer risks, and it will deliver a better solution in the long-term. • The supplier has a lot of experience and this new approach will definitely work.	Key benefits of the new approach • Limit risk to business continuity. • Better result overall, tailored to the needs of each department. • Less demand on resources during implementation. • Phased implementation costs. Next steps • Question and Answer. • List actions and responsibilities.

Figure 4.2 Story plan worksheet: case study 2—implant office support services company

entire presentation because the supplier has to set the scene for what they are going to go on to explain, that is, the context (Figure 4.2).

There are a lot of things wrong with the current approach, and these problems will need to be explained. However, the majority of the presentation is much more positive and covers the benefits to the customer if they agree to the new approach now being recommended by the supplier. In fact, bullet points 2 and 3 ("Proposed new approach in detail" and "Key benefits of the new approach") both allow the supplier to trumpet the positives of their new understanding and how it will benefit the customer.

The last point "Next Steps" has two purposes. The first is exactly as stated, to discuss what happens next. The second purpose is to provide the opportunity for the customer to affirm their support for the new approach, which is crucial to whether the supplier will be allowed to stay in the pitch. If the customer accepts the supplier's analysis, all well and good. Clearly, if the customer doesn't, the supplier will likely be thrown out of the pitch altogether.

Summarizing the Story Plan

Writing the Story Plan enables the supplier to test whether it flows logically from start to finish as it moves from topic to topic. It is the logical next step from the Meeting Goal, which means it is easy to see whether the right topics have been covered. It is also possible to verbally explain (to write a narrative similar to what has been written about the previous case study) the thinking and how this Topic Running Order will work. The Story Plan can, therefore, be tested and understood by everyone in the pitch team.

The Meeting Goal and Story Plan are all activities that together create the story that will be articulated through a document, presentation, or pitch, based on the thinking and strategy developed in writing the Communication Objective.

These three steps are the groundwork for mastering the art of persuasion. They are the output of real and deep thinking that is necessary if the content (that will be created or adapted next) is to have the meaning and persuasive qualities the supplier intended.

The next chapter covers six real-world case study examples to show how several organizations have tackled a number of very different but common challenges.

Chapter 6 and the subsequent chapters are all focused on an aspect of delivery: Content, Style and Language, and Delivery itself. These are all focused on how the thinking devised in Steps 1, 2, and 3 are articulated to become dynamic, engaging, and persuasive communication.

Personal Insight

The idea to have a Story Plan that included a detailed content list came about because of the way senior management handled presentations to important customers at the final pitch, or rather mishandled them.

The role of senior management can sometimes be a bit ambiguous at these moments, especially if the pitch team is competent and know exactly what they are doing. The reason the senior management are there at all is because they want to signal how important the customer is. Beyond that they don't have a role. So, what happened to make it necessary to detail content?

I imagine you might guess. Senior management will kick things off and do a brief introduction. The plan is for them to speak for a few moments before handing over to the rest of the team.

However, that isn't how it works out. Once they are on their feet in front of the customer, the plan goes out of the window. Emboldened by the moment, and remembering how long they've been in the business, they feel now is the time to reminisce, and so the minutes pass.

The idea had been to talk for 25 minutes, or so, to leave time for questions and discussions. By the time senior management have finished nearly 15 minutes have gone, and the brains of the rest of the team are working furiously to think how they are going to handle the rest of the meeting.

This is not that unusual, and is common for management, especially the most senior management, to go off-piste, which is where the content list comes in. By detailing every point that will be covered, it is much easier to brief senior management, to discuss with them what needs to be covered at the meeting, and get their agreement to speak for a short time. Without the detail, it is much harder!

Of course, overrunning isn't something done only by senior management, so the plan works for everyone.

CHAPTER 5

Case Studies

The following pages contain six case studies which are based on real examples taken from a number of consultancy projects. The case studies focus on the challenges facing six different suppliers, all of whom work in different industries, and are preparing for meetings with a customer at key stages of the sales process.

Case Study 1—Medical Instrument Manufacturer

Scenario—Positioning to Service the Customer's Current and Future Plans

This case study shows how profiling can have a significant impact on the way a supplier positions themselves. On researching the customer, the supplier learns that the customer is in negotiation to buy an American competitor. They see the potential of being able to service the customer in the future in the new territories and recognize this might help to win the current contract, which is only focused on the customer's current business footprint.

Case Study 2—Implant Office Support Services Company

Scenario—Changing the Delivery Strategy

This case study describes the situation where a supplier realizes their assumptions have led them to propose an unworkable solution, and therefore, they now need to change their entire approach if they are to be successful. The question for them is, how should they present this to the customer?

Case Study 3—IT Solution Provider to the Public Sector

Scenario—Challenging Customer Misconceptions

In this case study, the supplier recognizes their biggest obstacle to winning is that their customer doesn't appreciate the extent of their capabilities. Unless they can challenge current perceptions that they are too small to meet the requirements the customer has set out, they stand little chance of winning.

Case Study 4—Confectionary Packaging Industry Supplier

Scenario—Addressing Customer Relationship Issues

In this case study, a supplier has a relationship problem to deal with. The relationship between the leader of their customer service team and the customer has ceased to work well. They may need to change the team leader in order to build a more positive (and potentially winning) relationship with a customer.

Case Study 5—Technology Solutions Provider to the Finance Sector

Scenario—Pitch Strategy: Cost Savings or Realistic Outcomes?

This case study describes the scenario faced by a software supplier whose analysis shows how the solution they have proposed will both save money but also lead to redundancies, and how they prepare for the final presentation to a broad management team, including the department heads who will lose staff if the project goes ahead.

Case Study 6—Insurance Services Company

Scenario—Pitching to Retain a Service Contract

This case study describes the approach taken by the incumbent insurance services supplier whose customer has put the service they provide out to tender.

Case Study 1—Medical Instrument Manufacturer

Scenario—Positioning to Service the Customer's Current and Future Plans

The supplier is a global medical instrument manufacturer tendering to provide testing equipment and support services to a large pharmaceutical company with manufacturing sites in a number of countries in Europe.

The customer has issued a request for proposal (RFP) for a major contract and invited the supplier to put forward a proposal. One of the key requirements raised in the RFP is the importance of the supplier having a proven track record in delivering remote diagnostic services as part of a broad technical support package. It is clear the package is extremely important to the customer, who has explicitly requested the supplier is able to provide on-site engineering services rapidly, if required, and that service will be governed by short response and fix turnaround times to be covered in contractual service level agreements.

Following an initial briefing, attended by other suppliers and a meeting with the procurement department where they presented their company credentials, the supplier has made it onto the shortlist of suppliers and been asked to come to the European headquarters to present their solution to senior management.

On researching the customer, the supplier came across a news story on a business news portal that reported the customer was in negotiations to buy an American competitor, which has manufacturing facilities in the United States, as well as across Asia (Figure 5.1).

The RFP is focused only on purchasing equipment and services in Europe and has made no mention of the U.S. acquisition. However, since the supplier has offices in the United States and Asia, as well as Europe, it sees the potential of being able to fully service the customer in the new territories as well, should the acquisition go ahead. It is, therefore, important the customer recognizes their full global capabilities.

Although the expansion of the customer's business footprint may lead to a future business opportunity for the supplier to supply these new territories, whether they can use this knowledge to help them to differentiate themselves from other companies involved in the current tender depends on them being able to discuss the acquisition with the customer.

COMMUNICATION OBJECTIVE PLAN CASE STUDY 1 – MEDICAL INSTRUMENT MANUFACTURER	
Change Drivers	**Communication Strategy**
• The customer is in negotiations to buy a company in the US, with manufacturing capabilities in the US and Asia, where the supplier also has offices. The customer may, therefore, need additional services in both new territories, in the near future.	• Focus on the supplier's capabilities to supply and support the customer's European and Asia plants immediately. • Show how the supplier will be able to quickly service new territories (including new plants in the US and Asia) should the customer require them to. So, as the customer's business grows, the supplier will be able to fully service their requirements.
Top Customer Requirements	**Benefits/Key Features to Communicate**
• High quality instruments.	• Meets all US and European manufacturing standards. • Track record and history solely as a medical instrument manufacturer, with significant and proven Research and Development capabilities.
• Diagnostic support capabilities.	• Award-wining diagnostic tools are integral to the technology solution. • Automatic configurable alarm triggers support response. • Sophisticated fault diagnostic tools.
• In-country engineering and support services.	• Strong technical capabilities in country, with a proven track record. • On-site engineers work closely with Research and Development who also have access to top engineers.

Figure 5.1 Case study 1—Communication Objective Plan

As they prepare for the pitch and complete the Meeting Goal, the supplier is mindful that it isn't clear how much information about the acquisition is in the public domain, and they don't want to do anything that potentially damages the relationship with the existing European-based customer. Therefore, the team needs to be careful they don't pitch to provide a service that hasn't been requested by the customer. However, that doesn't mean they shouldn't communicate their global capabilities (Figure 5.2).

A key focus of the presentation will be to reassure the customer that the supplier has the capabilities to provide excellent service and meet the SLAs set by the customer. However, the approach being taken in terms of support is out of date in terms of the way new technology is being manufactured with a number of features that handle self-diagnosis, automatic alerts to the supplier's support desk, and can be replaced and swopped out easily and quickly. It is important to get this across.

Also, in respect of the element of caution about the pending acquisition, rather than overtly talk about this to the customer, the plan is to showcase how the supplier has a global footprint that already supports customers; and this will provide the opportunity for the pitch team to point out how they already run global services for other customers effectively.

MEETING GOAL
CASE STUDY 1 – MEDICAL INSTRUMENT MANUFACTURER

Gaps in a Customer's Knowledge	Perceptions to Challenge
• The customer's acquisition strategy might not be common knowledge, or even known to the stakeholders involved in this pitch. • The supplier's capabilities to service their requirements in the US and Asia, if the acquisition goes ahead.	• Since the customer seems to be exceptionally concerned with support, especially local engineering on-site support, it is important to reassure them they have the strength and depth to support the customer properly. • The support model, depending on on-site services, is as crucial as the customer thinks it is. Many of the new instruments have capabilities that accelerate problem diagnosis and swopping out devices is now common and an effective working practice.
Topics for Discussion	**Positioning**
• How some instruments are IOT enabled (Internet of Things). • Remote diagnostic capabilities and how this works worldwide. • Engineering capabilities in country.	• How the technology-build approach addresses many standard support challenges automatically, thereby reducing the requirement for on-site engineering support. • Having a blend of remote and on-site engineering services is standard practice and works well for other customers.

Figure 5.2 Case study 1—Meeting Goal

The meeting will provide the opportunity for questions and answers, and the acquisition may be something that comes up then, in which case the supplier will be able to explain how it can develop the services currently under discussion to cover new territories very quickly and easily, if that is what the customer needs them to do (Figure 5.3).

STORY PLAN WORKSHEET
CASE STUDY 1 – MEDICAL INSTRUMENT MANUFACTURER

Topic Running Order	Content List

• How some instruments are IoT (Internet of Things)-enabled.
• Remote diagnostic capabilities and how this works worldwide.
• Engineering capabilities in country.
• Summary.
	How some instruments are IoT enabled
	  • Explain IoT and how this is built into a number of key devices and instruments and is a growing trend.
	  • Show the process for automatic fault alert and reporting.
	  • Case Study: U.S.-based customer.
	
	Remote diagnostic capabilities and how this works worldwide
	  • Show live diagnostic dial-in software capabilities.
	  • Case Studies: European and Asia-based customers.

Key Messages	Engineering capabilities in country
	  • Go through the engineering services organization by country.
	  • SLA example reports.

• The customer has the engineering capability to service the customer and meet SLAs.
• New technology is transforming support, fault diagnostics, and maintenance approaches, and making them much more effective.
• The supplier is leading the way in IoT.
• The supplier operates worldwide and has the capabilities to fully service the customer's needs in full.
	Next steps
	  • Explain transition planning template to take on services from other manufacturers.
	  • Question and Answer.

Figure 5.3 Case study 1—Story Plan worksheet

Supplier 2—Implant Office Support Services Case Study

Scenario—Changing the Delivery Strategy

The company provides implant office support services to major corporations, which requires them to put staff on the ground in the offices of their customers to deliver a number of back-office services. The supplier was asked to respond to a tender document which, as normal, detailed the requirements of the customer. Since then, they have had a number of face-to-face meetings which led them to recommend a solution and outline a transition plan.

As they have got to know the customer better, what has become clear to the pitch team is that their approach is flawed. They made a number of assumptions that have turned out to be incorrect. This is a situation where, if they could turn the clock back, they would have tackled things very differently. However, they are where they are. They can, of course, keep going, but it is unlikely that what they have proposed can be delivered successfully (Figure 5.4).

This isn't the first supplier to jump into answering a brief from a customer without doing their homework properly. Changing direction is a brave move and one that could be a make-or-break moment. The supplier

MEETING GOAL	
CASE STUDY 2 - IMPLANT OFFICE SUPPORT SERVICES COMPANY	
Gaps in a Customer's Knowledge	**Perceptions to Challenge**
• The customer's original approach was to roll out implant services throughout the company in one go. What they haven't taken into account is the level of customization that will be necessary to ensure services work effectively in each department.	• The supplier's response to the customer's brief was based on previous solutions they provided to other customers. This was a mistake. Now it is clear the proposed approach will not work, the supplier needs to bring the customer with them in changing their approach, without losing credibility.
Topics for Discussion	**Positioning**
• Problems with current approach. • The revised project plans. • Benefits of the new plan in terms of risks, resources, and costs.	• The supplier has identified a better approach than originally proposed, which has a number of significant benefits. • Changing the approach will lead to much more effective and tailored implementation plans for each department.

Figure 5.4 Case study 2—Meeting Goal

STORY PLAN WORKSHEET	
CASE STUDY 2 – IMPLANT OFFICE SUPPORT SERVICES COMPANY	
Topic Running Order	**Content List**

• What is wrong with the current approach?
• Proposed new approach in detail.
• Key benefits of the new approach.
• Next steps.
	What is wrong with the current approach?
	  • Explain Current Approach.
	  • Go through the analysis of the current approach in terms of risk profile, the challenges of resourcing the project currently, and how the approach makes it difficult to meet the needs of every department.
	  • Summarize issues and problems.

Key Messages	Proposed new approach
	  • Proposed approach to pilot one department and apply learnings in a phased roll-out.
	  • Timing and delivery plan.
	  • How this will change project staging costs.

• The supplier's primary concern is to ensure the project is successful. They could keep going, but this is not in the customer's best long-term interests.
• For this to be the start of a meaningful partnership the supplier needs to be truthful and tell the customer what they really think.
• There are a number of benefits to the approach the supplier is now proposing, and fewer risks, and it will deliver a better solution in the long-term.
• The supplier has a lot of experience and this new approach will definitely work.
	Key benefits of the new approach
	  • Limit risk to business continuity.
	  • Better result overall, tailored to the needs of each department.
	  • Less demand on resources during implementation.
	  • Phased implementation costs.
	
	Next steps
	  • Question and Answer.
	  • List actions and responsibilities.

Figure 5.5 Case study 2—Story Plan worksheet

is going to have to admit they got things wrong from the start. The question is what the customer will make of it? They could react badly, think the supplier has wasted a lot of their time, and exclude them from further participation in the tender process.

However, there is a potential upside. What if the customer sees this positively? What if, although no doubt unhappy the supplier has made a mistake, they actually appreciate their honesty? Could it be a very positive move, even a game changer, that transforms the relationship from one that has faltered into a winning one? (Figure 5.5).

Supplier 3—IT Solution Provider to the Public Sector

Scenario—Challenging Customer Misconceptions

This supplier provides IT solutions to the public sector and is mid-tier in size with a good track record. The customer is looking for someone to provide hosting and software services, and the supplier has discussed their requirements on a number of occasions. The supplier has all the technical

MEETING GOAL	
CASE STUDY 3 - IT SOLUTION PROVIDER TO THE PUBLIC SECTOR	
Gaps in a Customer's Knowledge	**Perceptions to Challenge**
• Conversation with the customer is focused on company history and scale rather than on the supplier's capabilities to deliver the required solution. The advantages the supplier has, in terms of the way it can adapt to challenges that occur throughout a project and the involvement of management, are not fully understood or appreciated by the customer.	• The customer has a "big-is-best" mentality, and it is clear they favor the larger suppliers.
Topics for Discussion	**Positioning**
• Affirm how the supplier will deliver the project in full. • Use case studies to affirm the key benefits that differentiate them from their competitors.	• The supplier isn't the biggest company, but they are growing quickly because they are extremely good at delivering excellent service. • There is a perception that it is advantageous to be bigger, however, that can also create its own difficulties that are not in the best interests of the customer.

Figure 5.6 Case study 3—Meeting Goal

accreditations required (e.g., from Microsoft and others), so there should be no suggestion they are unable to deliver the requirements in full. However, it has become clear to the supplier that the customer doubts whether the supplier has the scale to deliver what is required and favor the larger companies who have also been invited to pitch.

This is not the first time the supplier has met this obstacle. They know they are a smaller and younger business compared to the bigger blue-chip competitors they are up against. Inevitably, that means they have less experience to demonstrate and fewer case studies to put forward to reassure the customer.

However, they also know they have a number of advantages over some of the larger competitors. They have a track record of delivering solutions quickly and outperforming many key performance indicators, and they have won contracts before from customers when up against larger companies (Figure 5.6).

This is problem that has been around forever. How does a smaller challenger brand reassure the customer that they are large and experienced enough to do the job? The only way for the supplier to challenge the customer's current perception is to openly discuss their concerns and use that discussion to get across the benefits and advantages they think they have compared to the larger companies (Figure 5.7).

STORY PLAN WORKSHEET	
CASE STUDY 3 – IMPLANT OFFICE SUPPORT SERVICES COMPANY	
Topic Running Order	**Content List**
• Project scope, deliverables, and timings. • Case Studies, one demonstrating agility, the other on management continuity. • Summarize key points.	Project scope, deliverables, and timings • Go through the list of project deliverables and how each one will be achieved. • Go through the timings for each stage of delivery. Case Study 1 • Focused on demonstrating the benefit to the customer of having senior management directly involved in delivering a project. • However desirable it is to anticipate issues and problems when planning a project, not all issues can be predicted. One of the significant advantages this supplier has in involving senior management throughout the planning and implementation of a project is how it enables them to adapt when things don't go to plan. • This case study shows how the supplier's project team were able to adapt the plan and reorganize resources to overcome unforeseen problems, and still deliver to the original project timeline. • The message of this case study is that by having senior decision makers directly involved in the detail of a project, it meant the supplier understood what was going wrong more quickly and were therefore able to put together an effective plan to mitigate issues much faster.
Key Messages	
• There are significant benefits to having the management team, who are involved in the pitch, also being involved in delivering the project. • They have beaten larger competitors to contracts precisely because they are more agile and able to solve problems that occur throughout the life cycle of a project. • Selecting the supplier isn't a risk for the customer.	Case Study 2 • Focus on demonstrating the benefit of having continuity in terms of key technical expertise throughout a project. • Knowledge and expertise are key to delivering every project. There are, therefore, significant benefits of having the same team assigned to project throughout its life cycle. Team continuity allows the supplier detailed knowledge about the customer which is a real strength and has tangible benefits in terms of problem solving, and the speed of delivery. • This case study shows how, part way through a project, the team recognized it was possible to run a number of activities concurrently, particularly in respect of data mining and analysis, that had originally been planned in series, shortening delivery timescales. • The message of this case study is that there is sometimes easier for the smaller company to ringfence key members of a project team, and this can be highly beneficial for the customer. Summarize key points • Go through key learnings from each case study.

Figure 5.7 Case study 3—Story Plan worksheet

Supplier 4—Confectionary Packaging Industry Supplier

Scenario—Addressing Customer Relationship Issues

This supplier provides packaging solutions to the confectionary industry and is involved in what has turned into an extended pitch process that has

MEETING GOAL	
CASE STUDY 4 · CONFECTIONARY PACKAGING INDUSTRY SUPPLIER	
Gaps in a Customer's Knowledge	**Perceptions to Challenge**
• The current team leader is experienced and skilled, and an asset to the customer. However, they don't need to be the main point of contact for the customer. Even if they take a step back and someone else takes over as key contact, they can continue to contribute to delivering great service, and importantly their knowledge and experience won't be lost.	• The supplier wants to signal they are aware and concerned that recent discussions have been awkward, and points that would normally be straightforward have become contentious.
Topics for Discussion	**Positioning**
• Review recent meetings. • Review the current team structure and personnel to test whether it meets the customer's current expectations and with a view to discussing the customer's feelings about the current team leader. • Discuss changing the leadership of the service delivery team.	• Addressing people issues is always difficult. However, it is important that the relationship works. The supplier is naturally concerned that things aren't going as well as they might, and it is worthwhile discussing whether a change of personnel is the right thing to do.

Figure 5.8 Case study 4—Meeting Goal

been stopped and started by the customer on a number of occasions for various reasons. The primary customer is a senior manager who is responsible for manufacturing on multiple sites and is someone with whom the supplier will have to work very closely on a daily basis if they are appointed. Due to the length of time, the pitch process has been running they have got to know the manager well and until recently felt they had built a good relationship.

However, recently it has become clear that the relationship between the customer and the leader of the supplier's customer service team has ceased to work well. Given it is clearly essential to have a strong and positive relationship with the customer, the supplier is concerned this will prevent them winning, unless they address the problem (Figure 5.8).

When service delivery is rooted in people relationships, it is essential for both the customer and supplier to get on. This isn't about friendships, although that can happen over time. It is more about the chemistry between people, especially at a leadership level.

There will be times when things go wrong, and that is when the supplier needs a strong customer relationship to fall back on. If at this early stage the chemistry isn't working, then it has to be fixed. Unless they do something, the supplier is very unlikely to win, especially as the key

STORY PLAN WORKSHEET CASE STUDY 4 - CONFECTIONARY PACKAGING INDUSTRY SUPPLIER	
Topic Running Order	**Content List**

• Review recent meetings.
• Review the current team structure and personnel.
• Discuss who would become the next team leader, if appropriate.
	Review recent meetings.
	  • Review the minutes from recent meetings. Discuss progress and whether the customer is happy with what is being done.
	
	Review the current team structure and personnel.
	  • Review the organization chart showing the supplier's customer service team.
	  • Double check whether this remains fit for purpose.

Key Messages	Discuss who would become the next team leader, if appropriate. • Discuss the role of team leader, and whether the current team leader should take a step back; in which case, discuss their successor.
• Reiterate the supplier's commitment to customer service and why this is a key ingredient in the success the supplier has had with other customers. • Express how the supplier is committed to making sure the customer has the best team working on its account and is not afraid to change the team, or enhance it, as and when required.	

Figure 5.9 Case study 4—Story Plan worksheet

decision maker is also the customer with whom they perceive there to be a problem (Figure 5.9).

Supplier 5—Technology Solutions Provider to the Finance Sector

Scenario—Cost Savings or Realistic Impacts?

This supplier provides technology solutions to the finance sector whose customer, an international partnership based in over 25 countries, is looking to source a new IT solution to replace an outdated finance and time-management system. As well as integrating with a number of legacy systems, the new system will need to ingest and process large volumes of historical data. Analysis shows the new technology platform will streamline current processes and increase efficiency significantly. However, it will also lead to some redundancies in a number of departments.

Achieving the benefits will not be straightforward. The success of the project requires the customer and supplier team to manage a major restructuring program. This includes a major redundancy program as well as implementing an entirely new suite of software tools that will change roles and responsibilities across the entire company in multiple countries. However, at the same time, the business needs to carry on as usual and there is a significant risk to business continuity.

The supplier's pitch team has reached the final pitch stage of a long procurement process. They have been asked to present to a large team of stakeholders, which includes senior management and the department heads who will be most affected by the changes. The supplier is concerned that not everyone has fully understood the work that will be necessary to implement the new system.

The question for the pitch team is where to focus? Do they headline the financial benefits of the project, thinking that management will like that message and appoint them; or do they go into the risks and the detail of delivering a project of this scale as well? They have managed similar projects before and believe demonstrating their expertise and experience is a key factor in being selected. However, they are worried that if they don't address the challenges facing the project team as a whole, and focus only on the headline benefits, they will lose credibility with the wider audience who are not only involved in making the decision but are also heavily involved in implementation.

This is a common conundrum facing many suppliers. Management can sometimes latch onto the headline benefits and play down the scale of the work that will be required to achieve them.

The scale of the benefits in this case study, in part, reflects the customer's underinvestment in the past. They are now taking a big step forward, which will enable them not only to catch up with competitors but also to take a step ahead. However, no one should doubt the importance of implementation in the overall success of the project. Getting it right is essential. Getting it wrong could be disastrous.

The supplier not only has to talk about implementation in detail but also has to factor the resources needed to deliver the project accurately into any fee proposal, as well as having detailed the commitment required from the customer. This is the reality of the project, and it is clearly to the benefit of both parties that they share an accurate understanding of the scope and scale of the project (Figures 5.10 and 5.11).

MEETING GOAL WORKSHEET	
CASE STUDY 5 – TECHNOLOGY SOLUTIONS PROVIDER TO THE FINANCE SECTOR	
Gaps in a Customer's Knowledge	**Perceptions to Challenge**
• The business case for going ahead is clear. However, the benefits are dependent on a successful implementation. Failure to implement the project properly could threaten business continuity in the short term, which would have significant financial consequences. It would also push full delivery of the project back, perhaps by months, which would mean the partnership would not realize the financial benefits until much later than currently anticipated. • The customer needs to recognize the importance of choosing a supplier who is capable of managing the implementation properly is their top priority in the decision-making process.	• The analysis done by the customer, and verified by the supplier, has shown the new system will significantly reduce indirect and employment costs. However, the focus of top management has been on the headline benefits of efficiency and cost reduction. For the wider management team, however, although they accept the benefits are real, they are extremely concerned about implementation and the consequences for individual departments if things go wrong. It is therefore very important to ensure top management understand the importance of a successful implementation and the concerns of department heads. • Establishing an openness and realism about the challenge with everyone at the customer is important because it provides reassurance to department heads that the supplier understands the challenges they will face. Also, it is important to recognize this is the beginning of a new relationship. Working together successfully in the future will be much harder if the department heads think the supplier has deliberately over-promised and minimized the challenges, simply to win the contract.
Topics for Discussion	**Positioning**
• Benefit analysis of the entire project, so everyone understands how it will impact the business. • Impact of implementation on the wider business, including analysis of risks, effort, and resources. • Implementation plan in detail.	• The supplier has managed a similar project successfully before and wants to make sure all parties benefit from their experience and expertise in planning for success.

Figure 5.10 Case study 5—Meeting Goal

STORY PLAN WORKSHEET	
CASE STUDY 5 – TECHNOLOGY SOLUTIONS PROVIDER TO THE FINANCE SECTOR	
Topic Running Order	**Content List**

• Benefit analysis.
• Project impact.
• Implementation plan.
• Summary.
	Benefit analysis
	  • Restate the benefits.
	  • Present the most recent data and impact analysis for the customer as a whole, and for each department.
	
	Project impact
	  • Business process transformation.
	  • Changes to business structures (including headcount reduction).
	  • Roll out and data migration.
	  • Key risks.
	
	Implementation plan
	  • Resources required of the customer and supplier.
	  • Installation.
	  • Data.
	  • Training.
	  • Support.
	
	Summary
	  • Key success factors.

Key Messages	
• The move to a new business system will result in significant financial and operational benefits, but only if the implementation and transition plan works. • Having sufficient resource and expertise are the biggest challenges to the success of the project. • The total cost of ownership of the supplier's solution is very low. Once transition has been completed the customer will continue to benefit from low operational costs. • The supplier has helped a number of customers implement new systems of a similar scale and level of complexity, and therefore has relevant expertise and experience to deliver this project successfully.	

Figure 5.11 Case study 5—Story Plan worksheet

Supplier 6—Insurance Services Company

Scenario—Pitching to Retain a Service Contract

This supplier has provided insurance services to a large international corporate real estate customer for several years. As well as the insurance product itself, they also provide a back-office function that manages claims. They have been asked to pitch to retain the business in line with the customer's new procurement policy.

In recent years, the supplier's customer service team has changed substantially. The customer has also made a number of management changes too, and only recently appointed a new director to oversee the relationship with the supplier.

The customer has issued a brief asking the supplier, and several of their competitors, to put forward a proposal to supply the required products and services. The brief also asks suppliers to demonstrate innovative ideas as to how they could transform the efficiency and management of the insurance back-office services, and rather than manage the pitch process themselves have asked a specialist procurement consultant to run the process. The consultant has worked on several other pitches with the supplier, but they have never won a pitch managed by this consultant.

Overall, the supplier has provided an efficient and effective service. Service levels, as described in the current contract, have been met. The relationship is considered strong, but there was an occasion a year before when they had had to replace the customer service team leader after a falling out with the lead customer, who has also since moved on. There have also been a few complaints that the supplier hasn't always answered e-mails quickly enough. Also, the customer hasn't been fully using the online claims system, preferring to contact the supplier's customer service team manually.

Although, at face value, this is common challenge and might appear easy to solve, in many ways, it is really challenging. The big difference between being the incumbent supplier and a potential new one is that a potential new supplier can offer the earth. They can make claims about the way they will work and how good they will be, without taking any risks because the customer, unlike with the incumbent, has no experience of working with them.

For the incumbent, everything is the opposite. Everything they say about themselves or promise to do will inevitably be compared to the experience the customer has had of them during the current contract. Of course, there are advantages too. There will be an existing relationship to leverage, and the knowledge the supplier holds about the customer will be much more detailed and insightful than any prospective supplier can have (Figures 5.12 and 5.13).

MEETING GOAL	
CASE STUDY 6 - INSURANCE SERVICES COMPANY	
Gaps in a Customer's Knowledge	**Perceptions to Challenge**
• SLAs are a measure of service, but they are only ever indicative of the quality and commitment to a customer. There will inevitably be times when this customer would have liked a faster response to an e-mail. However, this in itself does not show a failure in service levels. On many occasions, the supplier has responded immediately, and there will have been occasions when it has not been possible to do so.	• If SLAs remain the only focus of discussion, then it will undermine the knowledge and experience of the supplier's customer service team. They have in-depth knowledge of every aspect of the customer's business and their needs. The customer needs to appreciate how changing to another supplier will deprive them of all this knowledge and other benefits of working together for many years. These are real and tangible aspects of the current relationship that cannot be replicated easily with a new supplier. • The teams on both sides of the relationship have changed for various reasons. Although the reason for the supplier changing the team leader stemmed from a breakdown in the relationship with the customer's former team leader, the supplier demonstrated good judgment and a willingness to act rapidly to remedy problems that were detracting from the relationship. This, if anything, should be viewed positively, not negatively, and the supplier would like to emphasize their willingness to do whatever is necessary to make sure service levels remain high, at all times.
Topics for Discussion	**Positioning**
• An objective review of the relationship as a whole, including SLAs, to ensure performance is understood and appreciated fairly. • Showcase specific projects that demonstrate how the deep knowledge and experience of the team has added value to the customer in recent times. • The future relationship is important. Present an analysis of the challenges facing the customer, based on the intentions signaled in the customer brief as well as analysis of other business challenges the team are aware of from day to day working. Set out a plan as to how the supplier will deal with the challenges and mitigate future risks; including proposals to change processes and proposed enhancements to the team. • Review the online claims system to demonstrate how using it effectively can deliver significant benefits to the customer's business. Put forward clear proposals to increase adoption across the customer's business. • Why choose us?	• The tender process being pursued by the customer seems to imply there is a need for a step-change in approach. However, the service currently provided has been very good, and there is scope to improve it further if the customer was minded to fully use the online claims system. The customer should be confident they don't need to change suppliers to achieve their goals.

Figure 5.12 Case study 6—Meeting Goal

STORY PLAN WORKSHEET	
CASE STUDY 6 - INSURANCE SERVICES COMPANY	
Topic Running Order	**Content List**
• Performance review. • What of the future? • Online claims system – how it can be used to enhance efficiency • Why choose us?	Performance review • Detailed KPI analysis • Performance not captured in KPIs • Showcase specific projects and challenges where the customer and the supplier worked closely together to deliver a good outcome. What of the future? • Analysis of the challenges facing the customer's business in the short and medium term. • How will the supplier address these challenges? • Recommended changes to current processes. • Enhancing the supplier's customer service team.
Key Messages	
• The supplier has provided a high-quality service, and on many occasions have responded immediately when asked to. The team are committed to support the customer in the future, and the deep knowledge they have is an extremely valuable asset. • The future relationship envisaged will enhance the relationship even further in terms of technology, people and skills, and more effective processes. • Some of these proposals address the customer brief. However, they are broader in scope and also address risks to the customer's business and are driven by in-depth analysis and insight that is a direct result of the length of time worked together. • If the customer is open to these proposals, the total cost of the service could be reduced, at the same time levels of service and efficiency could be significantly enhanced.	Online claims system • Review key features, including analysis of what are not currently used. • Demonstration. • Recommended action plan. Why choose us? • Summarize benefits detailed throughout. • Express the supplier's deep commitment to the customer. • Ask the customer to renew the contract.

Figure 5.13 Case study 6—Story Plan worksheet

CHAPTER 6

Step 4—Content

Content

This chapter and the chapters that follow are all focused on an aspect of delivery, as the supplier takes the groundwork and thinking from the Communication Objective, the Meeting Goal, and the Story Plan and applies it to creating documents, proposals, and presentations; and ultimately to the way they present live face-to-face or using video conferencing. This step, Content, is where the supplier pulls together the content that was detailed in the Story Plan.

As the supplier begins to develop documents and presentations, one obvious point to remember is that although businesses are managed using processes and policies, they are run by people.

People make the decisions. They analyze suppliers. They judge and compare what they are being offered against their requirements. They listen to the opinions of managers and members of staff around them, as well as to influencers they trust or consultants they have hired.

Customers are no different to people in the "ordinary" world, just because they work in a business. They have preferences, prejudices, opinions, likes, and dislikes, just as everyone does. It is obvious, therefore, that understanding people and factoring that understanding into communication should impact what is written or said by a supplier.

In thinking about writing a document or a presentation, one question the supplier needs to answer is this. Are customers one dimensional? Will the content and message delivered at a presentation be heard in exactly the same way by everyone in the room? Will everything that is written down be understood in the same way by everyone who reads it?

Think about the many proposals and presentations you, as a reader, may have written or delivered. Were they written without any consideration of the audience? Did you take the view that since you knew what the meeting was about, you approached it as though the audience was one dimensional? Did you think the content and message you communicated was going to be heard and understood by everyone in exactly the same way; and that was all there was to it?

Thinking an audience is one dimensional is a mistake. It may make it easier to put a document or presentation together, but this oversimplistic approach is less likely to be either effective or persuasive.

How Do You Understand a Customer Stakeholder?

Think about what is happening between a supplier and a customer, either at a presentation or when they read a proposal.

When someone is speaking at a presentation, the customer is engaging with the speaker using two senses, sound and vision. They listen to and process what is being said, and they look at and process everything that is visual, such as slides and props, as well as being also affected by the personal appearance and behavior of whomever is presenting.

Clearly, reading a document is a very different experience and much more cerebral. However, the way a document is written and the language it uses will have a significant impact on how information is processed and judged by the reader.

The way the brain processes sensory information is clearly very complex. The key fact, from a supplier's perspective, is to recognize that no one reads, sees, hears, processes, and comprehends information in the same way.

Processing written, verbal, and visual communication is conditioned. It is conditioned by the listeners' or readers' opinion, judgment, and experience, and it is as though they are absorbing it through a lens, which has two filters, one of which sees things rationally and the other emotionally (Figure 6.1).

The rational response will be greatly influenced by a person's role or job function. Objective rational thinking is motivated by the individual's area of expertise and a sense of professional responsibility to represent the interests of the department or function they lead or are a part of. In other words, their parochial responsibilities. The same attitude also applies, but not as strongly, in relation to the wider business they work for.

The emotional response is much more personally driven. Emotional thinking is centered on the impact of something on oneself and the people around an individual who are valued, appreciated, and liked. It is

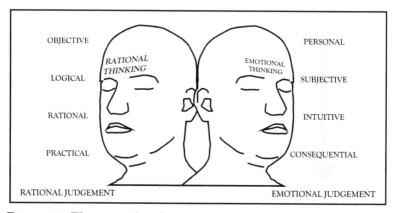

Figure 6.1 The rational and emotional thinker

commonly said that people don't like change, and this is true especially if whatever is changing has a direct impact on them. The emotional response is, therefore, much harder to predict or gauge because it is bound up in the way the individual feels about something.

Rational Thinking

How someone's job or role will influence their thinking can be demonstrated with an example.

Imagine the customer is a large global fast-moving consumer goods manufacturer (FMCG) that wants to replace an outdated system for managing the bill of materials (BOM) (the database that stores details about every component or part that is used to make its products) and its warehouse and stock control system. This is a large-scale project that will affect multiple manufacturing sites in multiple countries, and the company has set up a task force to run the project. The team of people involved represent each of the main functional departments.

Finance is focused on commercial terms, including the cost of licenses, support, installation, and maintenance. They are targeted to reduce operational cost and their focus is on the total cost of ownership of the new system versus a number of other systems it will supersede. The case for moving to a new system is very clear and will save the company a considerable amount of money. The system will work more effectively, but it will also require considerably less support from IT, and this in turn will reduce staffing levels in multiple sites across the company.

Their finance focus clearly is not on performance or operational impact, per se. There is a clear financial benefit, and they are in favor of the supplier whose costing model looks like it will be cheaper than anyone else. The area of greatest concern for them is the cost of transition and implementation, which are extremely difficult to quantify accurately and therefore have an impact on when cost savings will be realized by the business; and therefore, when they will be able to demonstrate, they have hit their cost reduction targets.

Operations have a very different mindset. They are the main sponsors of the project because they manage BOM and the warehouses. They will, therefore, be responsible for both systems, as well as for the performance of their global teams, who will handle the migration from the old legacy systems and also will use the new system on a daily basis. They are not against replacing the old systems, but in many respects, their daily work will not change significantly, although the new systems will be more efficient.

Their focus is practical, and how they will implement the system and transition data from multiple legacy systems while keeping everything running smoothly. In the longer term, they will need fewer people, but in the short term, they will need everyone currently in the teams as well as contactors to handle the volume of work. Therefore, another area of focus for departmental management is on how to manage current staff and staff retention.

What is very clear is that each stakeholder is focused on very different things, although they are part of the same project, and therefore, their concerns are completely different. It is easy to see how each stakeholder could disagree about almost every aspect of the project to the other, for entirely understandable reasons.

So, how does the supplier handle these differences? Because everyone is unique, every customer stakeholder will have their own interests and concerns when it comes to assessing a proposal from a potential supplier. Each stakeholder will be focused on their job and how the supplier's proposal will impact them.

Therefore, as documents and presentations are put together, the supplier needs to consider the different perspectives of the various stakeholders if they are going to communicate effectively with them all. What this means in practical terms is that they cannot treat the customer or an audience as though it is one dimensional. They need, instead, to determine the value and benefit argument from multiple perspectives.

How to Persuade a Rational Thinker?

Rational thinking is objective and is influenced most by logic and rational argument, which is assessed in terms of a professional interest (e.g., as a head of department) and the wider interests of the company they work for.

The focus of a rational thinker will be on tangible things, including costs, specifications, performance, reliability, and so on. They want to hear the reasons for doing something. They want to ask questions and receive detailed responses. Issues and challenges will need to be met with practical and realistic answers, with detailed explanations, and supported by robust, and reliable technology and processes. They may even recognize that there are some negative consequences of doing something, but still be supportive overall because they can see the broader benefits to the wider business are both logical and sensible.

The rational thinker will not be persuaded by spin or oratory. What this means for the supplier is that the more they put forward compelling, evidence-based reasons, and justifications in support of their proposal, the more likely they will persuade the rational thinker to choose them.

Emotional Thinking

The emotional response, by contrast, is inevitably much more personal. Emotional thinkers are subjective, motivated by a sense of self, by ambition, morals, scruples, and feelings. They may be driven by an assessment as to the consequences of decisions on things and people they personally care about, and they make decisions intuitively without feeling the need for logical arguments.

There will be a focus on consequence and what these consequences mean for them in terms of their daily work life. They will also be thinking longer term in terms of the implications for the wider business, and whether opportunities to advance their career will likely increase or diminish, as a result.

Because the emotional response is influenced by feelings and motivations, it is necessary to think more broadly than just about features and benefits and to think instead about how an individual is likely to respond to what is being written or presented.

How a supplier might approach communicating with a customer taking into account the emotional thinker can be demonstrated with an example, taken from Chapter 5, Case Study 5 titled Technology Solutions Provider: the scenario was Cost Savings or Realistic Impacts?

In this case study, the supplier, who provides technology solutions to the finance sector, is preparing to give the final pitch presentation. The proposal will have wide-ranging consequences for the customer, including a major restructuring program, redundancies, and roles and responsibilities being changed across the entire business. The pitch team were mainly concerned to ensure that the customer's management team did not underestimate the importance of managing the implementation carefully, if they wanted to realize project benefits.

This isn't just a rational challenge, but it is an emotional one too. The stakeholders, who will choose the supplier, represent every department, including those that will face major redundancies. In setting out the Meeting Goal, the perception the supplier wanted to challenge was a sense that they were not aware of how challenging this would be for the heads of department.

They recognized how important it was for the supplier to communicate to them that they understood the scale of the challenge and were concerned they would not be able to build a good working relationship if the customer's department heads thought the supplier had deliberately minimized the challenges ahead to win the contract.

This is good example of the supplier's pitch team considering the emotional response of key stakeholders before a presentation. The team recognize this is an important relationship that needs to work and aim to demonstrate empathy for the department heads who are going to face the most difficult challenge.

How Do You Persuade an Emotional Thinker?

The previous example describes an empathetic supplier, who recognizes the challenge ahead and the importance of the relationship with the customer to the success of the project. They want to be appointed by the customer, and therefore want to send a signal that they understand and are ready to support the key stakeholder, if they are selected.

Empathy and similar characteristics, such as rapport and affinity, understanding, awareness, and sensitivity break down the barriers between a supplier and a customer. The supplier who demonstrates these qualities is no longer on the other side of the table, but they stand alongside the customer, metaphorically speaking.

The emotional thinker, however, isn't always thinking the worst. There will be situations where a supplier is the bringer of great opportunity. Where a stakeholder sees the appointment of a supplier, and the changes that will ensue, as a really positive thing for them personally. Change can bring them promotion or increase their power and influence inside the customer.

Rational argument can feel unemotional and cold. Having the arguments, and the facts to substantiate them, is important. However, the dynamic of rational argument is neither collective nor co-operative. It is the supplier communicating their knowledge and expertise in a very direct way, as the subject matter expert. Alternatively, the supplier may take a much softer and more emotional approach, whereby they engage stakeholders as partners and also position themselves as collaborators.

Together, the supplier and the customer jointly come up with the best solution. When the supplier presents compelling reasons, they aren't claiming they have all the answers. Instead, they are acknowledging the role and value that has been played by the customer. Evoking ownership in the mind of the customer is very powerful, because they come to feel an emotional investment in what has been proposed. Therefore, as the solution and suppliers are considered, the stakeholder no longer regard the supplier as the outsider, but more as the informed insider.

Applying Rational and Emotional Thinking to Content Generation

The value of considering the stakeholder or the audience is to think through how content and the messages it communicates might be received by stakeholders, and whether this response will help or hinder the supplier wanting to be chosen.

Having a powerful case for the customer to choose a supplier because of the products, services, and solution being proposed is both a good thing and necessary. These are the arguments that will unquestionably convince the rational thinker, and the suppliers should be under no illusion that they will not get over the line with spin or oratory alone.

However, that does not mean that the emotional thinking side should be ignored. There are times when it will be more important to address the anticipated emotional concerns of a stakeholder than to bang the rational drum; and cultivating a more collaborative approach and recognizing the value of the customer's input in developing the solution strengthens the relationship considerably.

Having a clear view as to the best way of proceeding is something that needs to be decided early on, or the ideas simply won't be reflected in the content.

How to Test Whether Content Is Relevant

Having thought about the audience, the supplier will pull content together from previous documents or start creating afresh. However, it is worth remembering that this should be a process of distillation. There will always be more content available than can be covered at a meeting or included in a document or presentation.

Of course, all documents and presentations have constraints. Whether that it is the number of pages permitted by the customer or the length of time allowed to present. The key thing to remember is that everything must be relevant to the customer. It must follow the Story Plan, cover the agreed list of topics, and communicate the agreed key messages.

The mantra that "less is more" could never be more appropriate to a supplier pulling content together, and there are two tools that can also be used to help the supplier work more efficiently: the Three Cs and the So What Test?

The Three Cs

The Three Cs are Be Concise, Be Cohesive, and Be Coherent. These words should be engrained in the mindset of the supplier as they write or pull content together, and each one is explained in detail in the following subsections.

Be Concise

Being concise means being brief as well as comprehensive. Remember less is more! Neither audiences nor readers award contracts for long-winded presentations or documents. Long-windedness happens when authors try to cram in too much content and is a really common mistake. Inevitably, presenters run out of time or customers receive such overly long documents they can only skim-read them, if the supplier is lucky.

The watchword of good writing is being concise. State what needs to be said in a way that is short, punchy, and succinct. Therefore, be ruthless and delete content that is repetitive. ~~Once something has been said, it does not need to be said time and time again in a slightly different way.~~

Set realistic targets, whether a page count or word count, or timings for presenting each section of a presentation, and if the targets are exceeded keep editing until the document or presentation fits.

Be Cohesive

A document or presentation is the sum of its parts, and each part needs to fit together. Therefore, being cohesive means having a writing style and a standard look and feel.

There should be a consistency in the writing style, including a common dictionary of terms that includes acronyms, so the reader or the audience isn't presented with multiple approaches to expressing the same thing. Look and feel and the way information is presented should also be consistent throughout.

Clearly, if documents or presentations are created through a process of copy and paste, there is much more likelihood that the document won't be consistent, and it can take a lot of time to format pages, slides, diagrams, charts, and so on, so that they are cohesive. It, therefore, makes sense to invest time in building a library of materials that can be brought together easily, without compromising producing a cohesive end product.

Be Coherent

Being coherent means there is a logical flow to the document or presentation. Incoherent documents or presentations that are disjointed and jump around from topic to topic for reasons that are not apparent to the audience.

The result of chopping and changing is to make them harder to follow, whereas coherence makes sure every part a presentation is logical, smooth, and easy to follow. To help suppliers to do this, always remember: If it doesn't flow, it has to go.

So What Test?

The second is called the So What Test? The test applies equally to written documents, presentations, and scripts. The purpose is to assess whether what has been written is actually meaningful and relevant, or alternatively is superfluous and therefore an example of padding or a dysfunctional narrative.

Padding

Padding happens when a presentation or document contains content that doesn't need to be included. What this means is that it increases the volume or length of a presentation or document rather than the substance of it.

Examples of padding include long-winded sentences and explanations instead of short descriptions, statements that are repeated unnecessarily, often several times, and truisms, which are statements that really don't need to be said because they are so clearly obviously true to start with.

Dysfunctional Narratives

A dysfunctional narrative describes sentences or paragraphs that have no point or interest or value from the customer's perspective, or it is unclear what the point or relevance of it is.

Dysfunctional narratives include sentences and statements that are generic, superfluous, universal in application or relevance, sweeping, generalized, and cliches.

The best way to illustrate how the So What Test? can weed out unnecessary content is by example. The following three examples all fail the So What Test?

Example 1: "We (the supplier) have an international presence and are located in 16 countries around the world."

Does this pass the test? The answer is no! It fails because it is a dysfunctional narrative. It does not have a point of interest or relevance for the customer. It may be a statement of fact, from the supplier's perspective, but what is the relevance of this fact to the customer?

Imagine the customer is only based in one country. Why would this be relevant to them? The answer is it wouldn't be. Imagine the customer is based in 30 countries. Would this be relevant to them? The answer is that it depends where the supplier's offices are located in relation to the customers.

What would make the statement relevant is if it described the countries both parties were located in and explained why this is important and what value this brings to the customer.

Example 2: "Person X will be your account director. They will be responsible for your account and act as your primary go-to point on a daily basis. They will be in charge of the relationship and handle any questions you or the wider team have, and for coordinating the team back at headquarters to support you. They will also be supported by a team of experts, who will address technical matters, as and when you need them to."

Does this pass the test? The answer is no! It fails because it contains padding, as well as being a dysfunctional narrative.

The descriptions of the role of account director provides a good example of padding, because statement after statement is superfluous and repetitive.

- Persons X is "your account director."
- They are "responsible for your account."
- They are also "your primary go-to point" and "in charge of the relationship."

The meaning in the first three sentences could easily be expressed in one short sentence, "Person X will be your account director, and your primary go-to point."

It could also be argued that it is a truism, because being in charge of a customer relationship is what account directors do!

It is also dysfunctional because it does not tell the customer anything of value, beyond the job title. It would become relevant were the supplier to explain why this person will add value to the customer, perhaps in the context of their expertise and experience.

Example 3: "Our products are leading-edge and use state-of-the-art technology."

Does this pass the test? The answer is also no! It fails because the statement is a sweeping generalization or cliche. Everyone has "leading-edge technology." Can anyone imagine going to a customer and telling them they had "trailing-edge technology?" I don't think so!

Therefore, the statement has no real meaning or value to the customer.

Instead, the supplier has to assert the reasons why it is confident in its technology by pointing to particular relevant features that meet the customer's requirements or bring clear customer-centric benefits.

In Conclusion

Both the Three Cs and So What Test? are designed to help suppliers to focus on producing an end product, whether a document, presentation, or script; that is easy to follow, short, and punchy; and one that does not contain pointless, irrelevant, and time-consuming/page-consuming content.

Keeping sentences and paragraphs short and succinct and making them relevant to the customer adds considerably to the effectiveness of the communication. It makes sure the value and key messages the supplier wants to get across are clearer and therefore more compelling, because they won't be lost in the noise created by a long-winded document or blunted by statements that are simply irrelevant.

Personal Insight

One of the points I remember challenging at a pitch meeting with a large corporate law firm was about the way they wanted to express their longevity and experience to the customer. What started me off was the assertion that the pitch team had over "100 years of experience" which was asserted straight faced as real proof the customer would benefit enormously from their collective experience. From my point of view, the 100 years simply conjured up an image that somehow what had happened since Victorian times was somehow relevant to the customer now? What this image didn't do was assert anything of meaning to the customer. If the customer was going to be impressed by this number, then maybe we involved more older partners so we could get it up to 150 years! Wouldn't that even better, I suggested. What the supplier wanted to do was underline how the team being put forward had the right qualities to deliver excellent service to the customer. The three senior partners had between 17- and 38-year experience since qualifying, which is an average of 26-year experience. This was the value that counted. They had spent a quarter of a century delivering results for customer, and the message to this new prospective customer was that they would now benefit from this deep and relevant experience if they hired the firm.

CHAPTER 7

Step 5—Style and Language

By now, having followed the steps in the process from the start, the supplier will have written a Communication Objective, a Meeting Goal, and a Story Plan, the foundational thinking of become a Master of Persuasion.

In the last step, Content, they have pulled content for a document or presentation together, and carefully tailored it taking account of the audience and polished it to make sure it is concise, cohesive, and coherent, and removed padding and dysfunctional narratives.

The last two steps in the process, which are Style and Language, and Delivery, are focused on refining documents and presentations and on enhancing an individual's ability to perform and communicate in front of the customer.

Becoming a more persuasive communicator stems, in part, from understanding two of the most important ingredients of communication, words and style.

Words carry meaning and the style brings them to life. This combination is what makes writing and presenting so powerful and persuasive. The right balance of words and style can be transformative. It can take an audience to a completely different place through evoking an emotional response or being moving and uplifting, by painting a picture of the future and being inspirational, and by engaging the intellect by being thought-provoking. These states of mind are the result of the author or speaker's ability to engage an audience.

Of course, in business, content can be less emotional and more technical and informative, because the subject matter is focused on products, services, and solutions. However, it is a big mistake to think words and style used in business proposals and presentation don't matter or make an impact.

Business presentations inform, convince, inspire confidence, engender trust, and through logic, argument, and evidence lead a customer to believe a supplier is the best on for them. These are the transformations that persuade a customer to choose a supplier.

Assertiveness

Words conjure up images in the mind because they carry meaning, which is why it is important to choose them carefully. Being assertive is an important aspect of being persuasive, because the words chosen both reflect and convey the supplier's positive attitude and intent.

For example, it is easy to use model verbs such as might, could, and would without thinking about the meaning they communicate to the customer.

- Yes, a supplier *might* do something, or they might not.
- They *would* do something, if they can.
- They *could* do something, but that does not mean they will.

These verbs communicate intentions that are conditional on the supplier deciding to do something or finding a way to do something. They don't indicate real commitment. They don't inspire confidence, and they are not assertive.

Only when a supplier says they **will do** something do they mean they are committed to making it happen.

Some suppliers may feel that being assertive is similar to being bullish. They prefer understatement, modesty, and deference. However, being assertive does not mean the same thing. Bullishness, being aggressive, boastful, bombastic, and high-handed are not the qualities most customers want from a supplier.

They do, however, want suppliers who are confident in their own abilities, who will take responsibility for delivering products, services, and solutions that work, who will have a sense of duty to their customers, and who believe in themselves.

Solutions, services, products, and people are the substance of proposal documents and presentations, and the words a supplier chooses to explain themselves should not be chosen arbitrarily, as though their meaning doesn't matter. They should, instead, make it clear to the customer how they will meet requirements, offer the best performance, be cost effective, work hard, and apply their skills, expertise, and experience to delivering what the customer needs, alongside a host of other good reasons why the customer should choose them.

The words the supplier chooses to use, therefore, should positively affirm what they are proposing to the customer. They should present a view of themselves that is assertive, confident, and clear-sighted and leave no doubt or ambiguity in the mind of the customer that they are the supplier to choose.

Therefore, the purpose of editing proposals and presentations is to root out words that are misspoken, misleading, or ambiguous and to replace them with words that carry the supplier's serious intent. This is how the supplier asserts what they are proposing, why they are proposing it, and why they believe what they are proposing is the best solution for the customer, without hesitation, qualification, or doubt.

Simplifying Language

One of the golden rules of language is to use words an audience will understand. After all, if the audience doesn't understand what is written or spoken, then the impact of any document and presentation will be significantly undermined.

Simplifying language may be a golden rule, but how does it apply to technical detail? The more technical the subject matter, the more technical the language needed to explain it, and there comes a point where it is simply isn't possible to keep language accessible to everyone. Therefore, the supplier's pitch team need to consciously judge the level of technical detail they need to go into, based on their understanding of the audience who will be reading or listening; and the purpose of the meeting as set out in the Meeting Goal. Key to this decision is whether the technical detail is really necessary, or an example of grandstanding, and whether it passes the So What Test?

An even harder problem to crack is technical-speak, jargon, and acronyms. Almost every industry or sector has its own dictionary of words, terms, and acronyms that are professional shorthand, familiar, and completely understood by insiders and unfamiliar and opaque to outsiders. This, like technical detail, needs also to be carefully considered by the pitch team. One way to test this is to ask whether the audience fits into the author's or presenter's peer group? Do they share the same narrower ability, knowledge, and experience or do they represent a broader cross-section of the customer's business? The broader the audience, the better it is to avoid technical-speak.

Metaphors and figures of speech, including idioms, are also problematic for the same reasons as technical detail and technical speak. Dime a dozen, take a rain check, pull someone's leg, under the weather, a blessing in disguise, and so on. Idioms, by definition, are hard to work out because they are not literal. You either know them or you don't.

Business metaphors are a different kettle of fish altogether. A metaphor, by definition, is a figure of speech or phrase which is symbolic or representative but not literally applicable. Metaphors are borrowed from numerous sources, including sport, war, card games, cooking, and a host of general maintenance tasks. Therefore, the listener or reader has to be familiar with whatever activity the metaphor has been taken from, to understand what it means. Unless it is universal, it is quite likely it won't be immediately understood.

Some phrases have entered the world of corporate jargon, also called business speak, that are used to explain perfectly ordinary challenges and approaches to solving problems or delivering services. To some they are excruciatingly irritating or to others have become so banal they are meaningless. It's clear the supplier's pitch team, with limited time to engage a customer, needs to focus on the low hanging fruit, get their ducks in a row, and take their best ideas and run them up the flagpole, so they get the customer on the same page; otherwise, they are likely to let the grass grow. As a rule of thumb, corporate jargon, such as metaphors, are best avoided, but please don't shoot the messenger.

The serious point is that whether a member of the audience understands metaphors, idioms, and business jargon is down to their heritage, culture, age, first language, and personal experience. Also, language evolves and changes over time. Even within the same country, different generations invent new terms or redefine old ones, which can go on to mean something entirely different. If the audience comes from several different countries, then it is even more likely some won't understand what is being said, and more importantly, what it means.

Since communication is all about imparting information and ideas, and pitching is a step beyond that where the information is intended to persuade a customer to buy from a supplier, then whatever is said has to be accessible and understood by everyone the supplier's pitch team is trying to convince. Put yourself in the shoes of the audience and ask yourself whether they will understand what you are planning to say? Whether it is clear what you mean, and whether what you write or say is persuasive, and if you're in doubt, leave it out!

How to Avoid Inference by Saying What You Mean

Inference is a conclusion that is reached on the basis of evidence and reasoning. Therefore, if the supplier provides the evidence that what they are proposing will work really well and explain the reasons why a customer should choose them, it stands to reason, doesn't it, that they will be selected?

Of course, the problem is that the customer may not recognize what the supplier has inferred, or worse still, come to a conclusion that is, not only different but also damaging to the supplier's chances of winning.

The reason this might happen, in a way, is obvious. The customer is listening to a presentation or reading a document through their own eyes and ears. They don't know what conclusions the supplier has in mind. They process what is written or said completely independently and form their own conclusions.

It isn't only a problem in terms of information, capabilities, and product features, it is especially true of key messages. A key message, by definition, is not a simple statement because it is a complex idea or construct that is the sum of its parts, where several things are brought together to communicate something that is a core value of what the supplier has they offer. Therefore, the challenge for the customer is even bigger because they have to piece together lots of things to get the message.

Presentations or documents that only infer values, attributes, and capabilities but don't state them overtly are unlikely to be successful. For example, the benefit asserted by a supplier pitching to a customer which is an international business (quoted earlier in respect of a dysfunctional narrative) was that they too had offices in a number of countries.

"We (the supplier) have an international presence and are located in 16 countries around the world."

The problem with this statement, although it may be factually accurate, is that it doesn't pass the So What Test? because the value of this multicountry business footprint is not found in the knowledge of it. The value or benefit is apparent only when it is explained in terms of how having offices close to the customer will benefit them. In other words, the benefit is inferred, and it is up to the customer to work out the value for themselves.

In the mind of the writer, the meaning inferred is obvious, but that is, of course, because they know what it means. This is why it is so important for the writer to recognize when what is written is unclear—when they are inferring a benefit that hasn't been stated.

Therefore, the writer has to adopt the mindset of the audience. It is almost as though they need to forget what they inherently know about their own business or the benefits of the proposal or presentation they are writing. Instead, they have to continually ask themselves whether what they are communicating is clear, and whether the audience will get the message? If the audience will have to make the connections between what is being stated themselves, then it is up to the writer to replace inferences with clearly stated benefits, clear messages, and clear explanation.

Personal Insight

Working with my clients over a period of time really underlined how common it was for them to infer benefits and forget that what they were actually expecting the customer to do was to join the dots and make all the connections between what they were actually saying and the messages they wanted to communicate to the customer. The other common challenge was that quite a number of senior leaders didn't really think they needed to learn anything about communication at all! They already knew what they were doing. Therefore, overcoming the skepticism of some clients was what the first major task was all about!

So, I developed a way of testing how well they communicated. I'd ask a new client to take me through one of their recent pitches, not to present it, as such, but to go through it and explain what it was about and what important points were they communicating. Then, I'd ask them to identify each key message they had communicated to the customer, and I'd write them down on a white board, so we could refer back to them. Next, I'd ask the client to show me which part of the presentation communicated each message. In many cases, the messages simply weren't there. They weren't stated in any way at all. Yes, the client was making really relevant and important points, but they were, so often, leaving it up to the customer to join up a number of separate points into one idea or conclusion that underlined the supplier's skills and capabilities. Point made.

Inadvertent Disclosure

If inference is a problem because what is meant isn't stated, inadvertent disclosure is when a supplier discloses information to their own detriment.

In a sales context, this has always been an issue for someone who might be best described as a loudmouth or bigmouth, someone who is a bit of a show-off or braggart, who inadvertently tells the customer things that no supplier would ever choose to share.

However, beyond the maverick employee, this is actually a serious issue that is worthy of consideration by every supplier. One of the key points discussed in Chapter 6 on Content is how information is processed. How verbal and written communication is conditioned by the listener's or reader's opinion, judgment, and experience. Therefore, it is impossible for the writer or speaker to control how what they communicate is received by the customer. This, by definition, places a responsibility onto the shoulders of everyone in the supplier's pitch team, to think about the consequences of what they say or write to a customer, to ensure, as far as possible, that it is neither misunderstood nor misrepresentative.

This is very pertinent to the throwaway comment. The most obvious trap is for someone to share a view or opinion about the company they work for, or an individual in the pitch team. It is understandable why this might happen. People are critical, by nature. They will have an opinion of how a company is run. They may not have a strong relationship with everyone in the team, or with particular existing customers. Also, things happen, mistakes are made, things go wrong, and all of this can leak out if the supplier's pitch team are careless in terms of what they say.

But this does not apply to a person saying something completely out of order. It is more nuanced than that, when what is said seems innocuous but actually fundamentally undermines the values or principles the supplier says they hold dear.

For example, take a really simple thing, like a presentation where the slides contain typographical errors or include the name of a different customer. Unfortunately, the supplier didn't proofread the document properly. Maybe they were in a hurry? The speaker realizes the mistake in the middle of presenting and apologizes. They are embarrassed and make an off-hand remark about how everything is last minute and always done in a hurry. The problem is one of the key attributes the supplier is trying to promote is how quality is really important and how they always take care to make sure that everything is checked before being sent to the customer. The construct of quality is damaged by the off-hand remark.

Another example is IT, which is a common target to blame when things don't go to plan. How many times has a pitch team blamed their own company for not delivering something to the customer? The reason or excuse is that it's because IT never works properly, despite the number of times they have complained. As with the example about proofreading, this off-hand comment strikes at the heart of the value being projected by the supplier. Why would a customer choose to work with a supplier whose IT doesn't work properly?

In all likelihood, the off-hand remark is not a realistic or accurate assessment of the supplier. It is a response to a particular situation that is awkward to deal with, and where the easy way out is find something to explain the problem away or blame someone else. The problem is how this can be amplified to mean something much bigger.

Sentiment

Although a document or presentation has a structure (taken from the Story Plan) and content, that doesn't mean it will be written or presented dispassionately. The words and the style of a proposal or presentation are driven by a sentiment that is motivated by personal commitment, the opinion, feelings, and ambition of the writer and speaker, and what they want to evoke in the audience. That is why documents and presentations are engaging and persuasive; and others fall flat.

Sentiments are not constant. A document or presentation is not written with one sentiment throughout. Sentiments ebb and flow throughout a document or presentation depending on subject matter. The sentiment is chosen because of the response the author wants to elicit from the audience.

Therefore, parts of a presentation may be driven by a sentiment intended to motivate and inspire, whereas other parts may be driven a sentiment to provoke an audience to think, others may be more educational and informative.

Sentiment determines the words and style and needs to be chosen carefully depending on the subject matter and circumstances. In the context of pitching and persuading a customer to buy products and services, it is important to identify the right sentiment for the occasion and therefore match words and style that are both sympathetic and appropriate.

Knowing the intended sentiment should make it easier for a presenter or writer to choose the most appropriate words, and it also follows that the process and time spent refining documents and presentations together will get shorter and the end result will not only be better but also be more engaging and more persuasive too.

Sentiment is driven by four motivators. These are context, aspiration, information, and exposition.

Contextual sentiments are driven by events. From a communication perspective, this means that there is a focus on specific real-world factors, circumstances, or situations that a business needs to address in a document or presentation. When content is motivated by a contextual sentiment, the speaker or writer is having to explain why something needs to be done (Figure 7.1).

The reasons may be many and various. The business may have been forced to explain itself. It might empathize with a predicament, want to express appreciation to staff or the broader organization because of what they have done. It may feel it needs to apologize for something, or even defend itself from criticism. The point is that the content is motivated by a business context and that determines the choice of words and the style.

The opposite corner of the Style Block to contextual sentiments is aspirational sentiments. These are not motivated by real-world context or

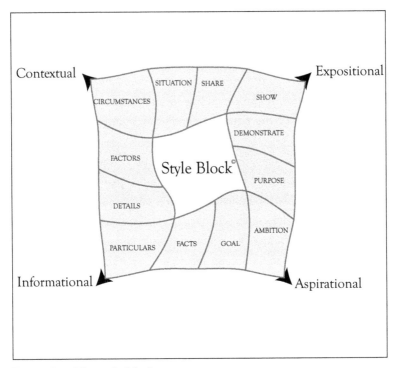

Figure 7.1 The style block

things happening now. Instead, they look to the future. Aspirational sentiments are focused on ambitions, or resolutions or intentions to achieve
something, on goals, and on targets. When content is motivated by an
aspirational sentiment, the speaker or writer is setting out their vision for
the future or what it hopes to achieve or what is possible. This motivation
similarly determines the choice of words and style.

Informational sentiments are completely different to both contextual
and aspirational sentiments, as they are rooted more in the real-world,
including products, services, and solutions, and focused on details,
particulars, and facts. When content is motivated by an informational
sentiment, the speaker or writer is explaining, educating, or providing
evidence with regard to capabilities, specifications, and processes. They
are, therefore, rooted in the practicality of things; and the words and style
will, therefore, be rooted there too.

Finally, expositional sentiments are the opposite of informational
ones. This sentiment is rooted in describing ideas, theories, and experi-
ences and focused on demonstrating, presenting, or showing something

off to an audience. When content is motivated by an expositional sentiment, the speaker or writer is demonstrating how something works or
divulging a personal experience or knowledge of something.

How to Apply the Style Block When Creating Content

The Style Block image shows the four motivators at the four corners of
a block. Each motivator drives the selection of words and style, and it is,
therefore, possible to show the characteristics of each sentiment, including the meaning intended and the verbs that reflect and are appropriate
to each sentiment.

The writer or presenter should select the sentiment that is the closest
match (contextual, aspirational, informational, or expositional) and then
work with the verbs displayed or similar verbs in order to express themselves appropriately.

Contextual Sentiments

Contextual sentiments have three drivers: situation, circumstances, and
factors, which are as follows (Figures 7.2–7.7):

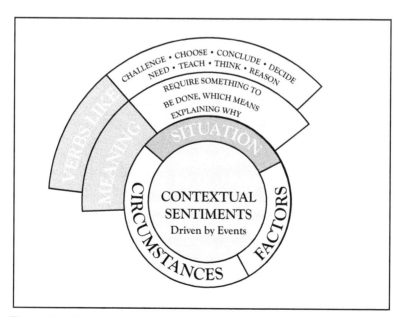

Figure 7.2 Contextual sentiments focused on situation

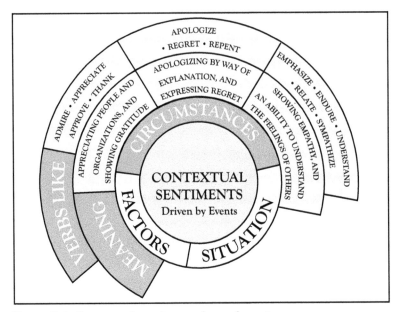

Figure 7.3 Contextual sentiments focused on circumstance

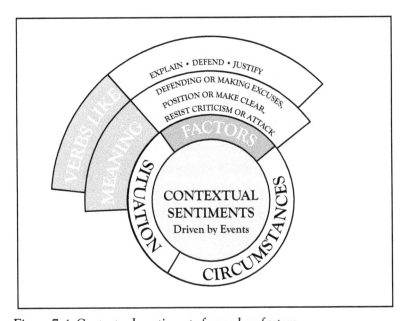

Figure 7.4 Contextual sentiments focused on factors

Aspirational Sentiments

Aspirational sentiments have three drivers: ambition, purpose, and goal, which are as follows:

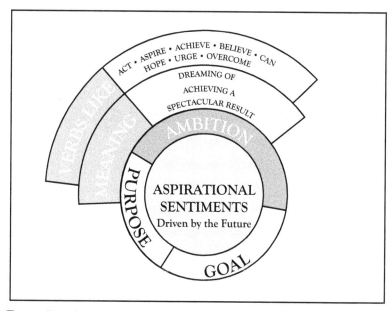

Figure 7.5 Aspirational sentiments focused on ambition

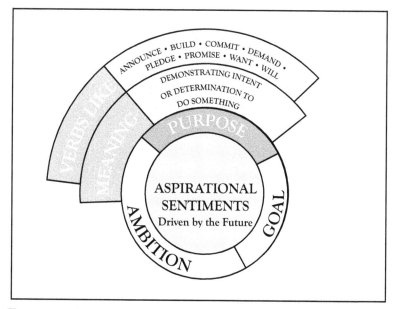

Figure 7.6 Aspirational sentiments focused on purpose

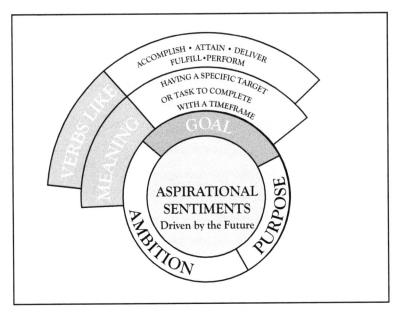

Figure 7.7 Aspirational sentiments focused on goal

Informational Sentiments

Informational sentiments have three drivers: details, particulars, and facts, which are as follows (Figures 7.8–7.10):

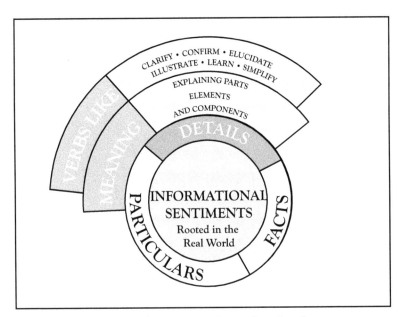

Figure 7.8 Informational sentiments focused on details

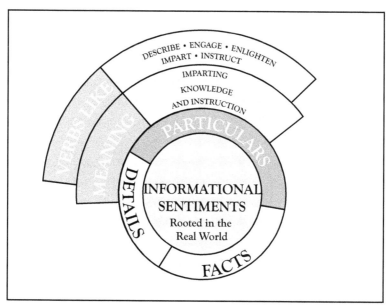

Figure 7.9 *Informational sentiments focused on particulars*

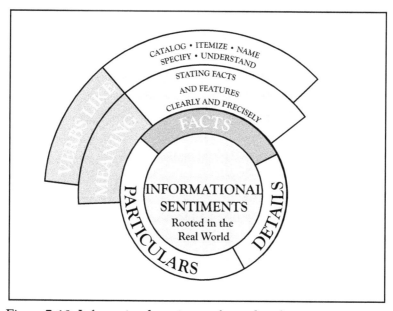

Figure 7.10 *Informational sentiments focused on facts*

Expositional Sentiments

Expositional sentiments have three drivers: demonstrate, share, and show, which are as follows (Figures 7.11–7.13):

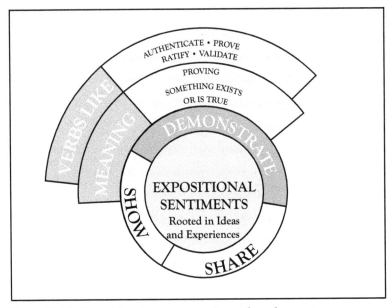

Figure 7.11 Expositional sentiments focused on demonstrate

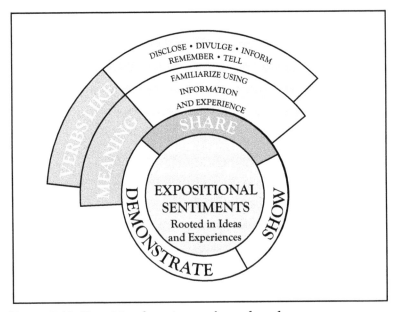

Figure 7.12 Expositional sentiments focused on share

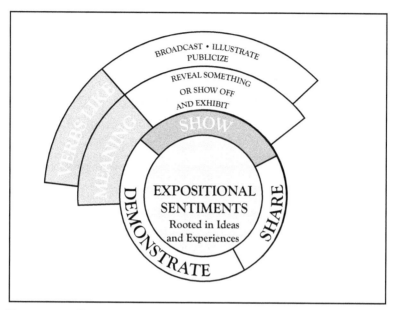

Figure 7.13 Expositional sentiments focused on show

Updated Case Study Example Story Plans Including Sentiment

Chapter 6 contained six case studies and showed real examples of how suppliers had tackled a number of business issues using the first three steps in the process of How to Become a Master of Persuasion. In the following pages, the sentiment that would drive each part of the Story Plan has been added (Figures 7.14–7.19).

STORY PLAN WORKSHEET (INC' SENTIMENT)
CASE STUDY 1 - MEDICAL INSTRUMENT MANUFACTURER

This is a presentation which focuses on explanation and details and is therefore is Informational. The first part, which deals with how IoT is transforming the industry is, however, is about the future and therefore Aspirational. The live demonstrate is designed to show the customer what is possible now, and the final part explains the transition plan and is also Aspirational.

Topic Running Order	Content List	Sentiment
• How some instruments are IoT (Internet of Things)-enabled. • Remote diagnostic capabilities and how this works worldwide. • Engineering capabilities in country. • Summary.	How some instruments are IoT enabled • Explain IoT and how this is built into a number of key devices and instruments and is a growing trend. • Show the process for automatic fault alert and reporting. • Case Study: U.S.-based customer.	• ASPIRE > Ambition > Dreaming of achieving a spectacular result > Believe • INFORM > Details > Explaining parts, elements, and components > Elucidate • INFORM > Detail > Explaining parts, elements, and components > Illustrate
Key Messages		
• The customer has the engineering capability to service the customer and meet SLAs. • New technology is transforming support, fault diagnostics, and maintenance approaches, and making them much more effective. • The supplier is leading the way in IoT. • The supplier operates worldwide and has the capabilities to fully service the customer's needs in full.	Remote diagnostic capabilities and how this works worldwide • Show live diagnostic dial-in software capabilities. • Case Studies: European and Asia-based customers.	• EXPOSE > Demonstrate > Prove something exists and is true > Prove • INFORM > Details > Explaining parts, elements, and components > Illustrate
	Engineering capabilities in country • Go through the engineering services organization by country.	• INFORM > Details > Explaining parts, elements, and components > Detail
	• SLA example reports.	• INFORM > Details > Explaining parts, elements, and components > Illustrate
	Next steps • Explain transition planning template to take on services from other manufacturers. • Question and Answer.	• ASPIRE > Goal > Require something to be done, which is Having a specific target or task to complete within a timeframe > Specify

Figure 7.14 Case study 1—medical instrument manufacturer Story Plan worksheet inc' sentiment

STORY PLAN WORKSHEET (INC' SENTIMENT)		
CASE STUDY 2 – IMPLANT OFFICE SUPPORT SERVICES COMPANY		

This is a presentation which focuses on explaining a major shift in approach. Therefore, the supplier has to explain the context of the situation, why the original approach is flawed, and the benefits of what they now propose. However, the proposed plan offers a number of significant benefits to the customer and will deliver a better result in the longer term.

Topic Running Order	Content List	Sentiment
• What is wrong with the current approach? • Proposed new approach in detail. • Key benefits of the new approach. • Next steps.	What is wrong with the current approach? • Explain Current Approach.	• CONTEXT > Situation > Requiring something to be done, which means explaining why > Necessitate
	• Go through the analysis of the current approach in terms of risk profile, the challenges of resourcing the project currently, and how the approach makes it difficult to meet the needs of every department.	• INFORM > Details > Explaining parts, elements, and components > Elucidate
Key Messages	• Summarize issues and problems.	• CONTEXT > Situation > Requiring something to be done, which means explaining why > Conclude
• The supplier's primary concern is to ensure the project is successful. They could keep going, but this is not in the customer's best long-term interests. • For this to be the start of a meaningful partnership the supplier needs to be truthful and tell the customer what they really think. • There are a number of benefits to the approach the supplier is now proposing, and fewer risks, and it will deliver a better solution in the long-term. • The supplier has a lot of experience and this new approach will definitely work.	Proposed new approach • Proposed approach to pilot one department and apply learnings in a phased roll-out. • Timing and delivery plan. • How this will change project staging costs. Key benefits of the new approach • Limit risk to business continuity. • Better result overall, tailored to the needs of each department. • Less demand on resources during implementation. • Phased implementation costs. Next steps • Question and Answer. • List actions and responsibilities.	• ASPIRE > Ambition > Dreaming of achieving a spectacular result > Achieve • ASPIRE > Goal > Having a specific target or task to complete within a timeframe > Fulfill • INFORM > Facts > Stating facts and features clearly and precisely > Itemize • ASPIRE > Ambition > Dream of achieving a specific result > Achieve • INFORM > Facts > Stating facts and features clearly and precisely > Catalog • INFORM > Facts > Stating facts and features clearly and precisely > Itemize

Figure 7.15 Case study 2—implant office support services Story Plan worksheet inc' sentiment

STORY PLAN WORKSHEET (INC' SENTIMENT)		
CASE STUDY 3 – IMPLANT OFFICE SUPPORT SERVICES COMPANY		
There should be no suggestion they are unable to deliver the requirements in full. However, it has become clear to the supplier that the customer doubts whether the supplier has the scale to deliver what is required and favor the larger companies who have also been invited to pitch.		
Topic Running Order	**Content List**	**Sentiment**
• Project scope, deliverables, and timings. • Case Studies, one demonstrating agility, the other on management continuity. • Summarize key points.	Project scope, deliverables, and timings • Go through the list of project deliverables and how each one will be achieved. • Go through the timings for each stage of delivery.	• INFORM > Facts > Stating facts and features clearly and precisely > Itemize • INFORM > Facts > Stating facts and features clearly and precisely > Itemize
Key Messages • There are significant benefits to having the management team, who are involved in the pitch, also being involved in delivering the project. • They have beaten larger competitors to contracts precisely because they are more agile and able to solve problems that occur throughout the life cycle of a project. • Selecting the supplier isn't a risk for the customer.	Case Study 1 • Focused on demonstrating the benefit to the customer of having senior management directly involved in delivering a project. (See full case study to reference full Content List) • The message of this case study is that by having senior decision makers directly involved in the detail of a project, meant the supplier understood what was going wrong more quickly and were therefore able to put together an effective plan to mitigate issues much faster. Case Study 2 • Focus on demonstrating the benefit of having continuity in terms of key technical expertise throughout a project. (See full case study to reference full Content List) • The message of this case study is that there it is sometimes easier for the smaller company to ringfence key members of a project team, and this can be highly beneficial for the customer. Summarize key points • Go through key learnings from each case study.	• EXPOSE > Demonstrate > Prove something exists and is true > Prove • INFORM > Details > Explaining parts, elements, and components > Illustrate • EXPOSE > Demonstrate > Prove something exists and is true > Prove • INFORM > Details > Explaining parts, elements, and components > Illustrate • INFORM > Details > Explaining parts, elements, and components > Illustrate

Figure 7.16 Case study 3—IT solution provider to the public sector Story Plan worksheet inc' sentiment

STORY PLAN WORKSHEET (INC' SENTIMENT)		
CASE STUDY 4 - CONFECTIONARY PACKAGING INDUSTRY SUPPLIER		
It has become clear that the relationship between the customer and the leader of the supplier's customer service team has ceased to work well. Given it is clearly essential to have a strong and positive relationship with the customer, the supplier is concerned this will prevent them winning, unless they address the problem.		
Topic Running Order	**Content List**	**Sentiment**
• Review recent meetings. • Review the current team structure and personnel. • Discuss who would become the next team leader, if appropriate.	Review recent meetings. • Review the minutes from recent meetings. Discuss progress and whether the customer is happy with what is being done.	• EXPOSE > Share > Familiarize using information and experience > Disclose
Key Messages	Review the current team structure and personnel. • Review the organization chart showing the supplier's customer service team. • Double check whether this remains fit for purpose.	• INFORM > Particulars > Imparting knowledge and instruction > Describe • ASPIRE > Purpose > Demonstrating the intern or determination to do something > Promise
• Reiterate the supplier's commitment to customer service and why this is a key ingredient in the success the supplier has had with other customers. • Express how the supplier is committed to making sure the customer has the best team working on its account and is not afraid to change the team, or enhance it, as and when required.	Discuss who would become the next team leader, if appropriate. • Discuss the role of team leader, and whether the current team leader should take a step back; in which case, discuss their successor.	• INFORM > Details > Explaining parts, elements, and components > Clarify

Figure 7.17 Case study 4—confectionary packaging industry supplier Story Plan worksheet inc' sentiment

STORY PLAN WORKSHEET (INC' SENTIMENT)
CASE STUDY 5 - TECHNOLOGY SOLUTIONS PROVIDER TO THE FINANCE SECTOR
The supplier not only has to talk about implementation in detail, but it also has to factor the resources needed to deliver the project accurately into any fee proposal, as well as having detailed the commitment required from the customer. This is the reality of the project, and it is clearly to the benefit of both parties that they share an accurate understanding of the scope and scale of the project.

Topic Running Order	Content List	Sentiment
• Benefit analysis. • Project impact. • Implementation plan. • Summary.	Benefit analysis • Restate the benefits.	• ASPIRE > Ambition > Dreaming of achieving a spectacular result > Achieve
	• Present the most recent data and impact analysis for the customer as a whole, and for each department.	• INFORM > Facts > Stating facts and features clearly and precisely > Itemize
Key Messages		
• The move to a new business system will result in significant financial and operational benefits, but only if the implementation and transition plan works. • Having sufficient resource and expertise are the biggest challenges to the success of the project. • The total cost of ownership of the supplier's solution is very low. Once transition has been completed the customer will continue to benefit from low operational costs. • The supplier has helped a number of customers implement new systems of a similar scale and level of complexity, and therefore has relevant expertise and experience to deliver this project successfully.	Project impact • Business process transformation. • Changes to business structures (including headcount reduction). • Roll out and data migration. • Key risks.	• INFORM > Details > Explaining parts, elements, and components > Clarify
	Implementation plan • Resources required of the customer and supplier. • Installation. • Data. • Training. • Support.	• INFORM > Facts > Stating facts and features clearly and precisely > Itemize
	Summary • Key success factors.	• ASPIRE > Goal > Require something to be done, which is Having a specific target or task to complete within a timeframe > Accomplish

Figure 7.18 Case study 5—technology provider to the finance sector Story Plan worksheet inc' sentiment

STORY PLAN WORKSHEET (INC' SENTIMENT)		
CASE STUDY 6 - INSURANCE SERVICES COMPANY		
This supplier has provided insurance services to a large international corporate real estate customer for several years. As well as the insurance product itself, they also provide a back-office function that manages claims. They have been asked to pitch to retain the business, in line with the customer's new procurement policy.		
Topic Running Order	**Content List**	**Sentiment**
• Performance review. • What of the future? • Online claims system – how it can be used to enhance efficiency • Why choose us?	Performance review • Detailed KPI analysis • Performance not captured in KPIs • Showcase specific projects and challenges where the customer and the supplier worked closely together to deliver a good outcome.	• INFORM > Details > Explaining parts, elements, and components > Confirm • INFORM > Explaining parts, elements, and components > Illustrate • EXPOSE > Demonstrate > Prove something exists and is true > Prove
Key Messages		
• The supplier has provided a high-quality service, and on many occasions have responded immediately when asked to. The team are committed to support the customer in the future, and the deep knowledge they have is an extremely valuable asset. • The future relationship envisaged will enhance the relationship even further in terms of technology, people and skills, and more effective processes. • Some of these proposals address the customer brief. However, they are broader in scope and also address risks to the customer's business and are driven by in-depth analysis and insight that is a direct result of the length of time worked together. • If the customer is open to these proposals the total cost of the service could be reduced, at the same time levels of service and efficiency could be significantly enhanced.	What of the future? • Analysis of the challenges facing the customer's business in the short and medium term. • How will the supplier address these challenges? • Recommended changes to current processes. • Enhancing the supplier's customer service team. Online claims system • Review key features, including analysis of what are not currently used. • Demonstration. • Recommended action plan. Why choose us? • Summarize benefits detailed throughout. • Express the supplier's deep commitment to the customer. • Ask the customer to renew the contract.	• EXPOSE > Factors > Defending or making excuses, position or make clear resist criticism or attack > Explain • ASPIRE > Purpose > Demonstrating the intent or determination to do something > Focus • EXPOSE > Share > Familiarize using information and experience > Inform • EXPOSE > Demonstrate > Prove something exists and is true > Prove • ASPIRE > Goal > Having a specific target or task to complete within a timeframe > Accomplish • INFORM > Explaining parts, elements, and components > Detail • ASPIRE > Purpose > Demonstrating the intent or determination to do something > Pledge

Figure 7.19 Case study 6—insurance services company Story Plan worksheet inc' sentiment

CHAPTER 8

Step 6—Pitch and Presentation

By now, the pitch team has a clear Communication Objective and has a clear Meeting Goal that will move them further along the sales process, closer to winning. A Story Plan has been written that identifies topics and a logical structure as well as the key messages the pitch team want the customer to hear and remember. Content has been refined in the light of the audience who will be at the presentation, and the words and style have been carefully considered and refined to ensure that the presentation evokes the appropriate sentiment and asserts why the supplier offers the best solution to the customer.

Delivering the presentation is step six and the finale of becoming a Master of Persuasion (Figure 8.1). It is the culmination of all the thinking, preparation, and refinement that enables the supplier to be an effective and persuasive communicator.

It is now time for the team to pitch the story that has been carefully crafted to the customer. Being good on one's feet and a confident and capable speaker are goods skill to learn. To be effective in front of a client requires the presenter to think about the way they project themselves, how they bring the story to life using their voice, and how they perform and physically engage the audience.

However, presenting is not the same as acting. The speaker doesn't need to play a part, as though they are in a play or a film. In many respects what counts more, from the customer's perspective, is for a supplier's pitch team to be authentic. After all, the big difference between performance and reality is what happens after it has finished.

The audience in a theater watching a film will go home. They can acknowledge the quality of performance and the spectacle, but that is it.

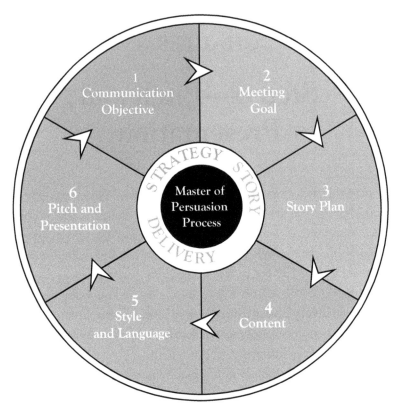

Figure 8.1 The process of persuasion

In business, the customer works with the supplier's team, and often in a close relationship. Therefore, approaching presenting as a performance completely misses the point.

Many customers want the team they will work with to be involved in the pitch. They want to ask the people who will do the work to answer questions and explain how they will solve problems and deliver service and support.

This is especially true of the supplier's team involved in technical matters, where a key element of what the customer is buying is expertise. Being a good communicator is always going to be important, but having trust and faith in the supplier's team in terms of their competence and ability to provide reliable and useful advice far outweighs any presentation polish.

How to Behave (Physically) in Front of an Audience

Some of the points in this section apply to presenting online using video conferencing, and there is a section specially addressing the challenges this poses.

The way a speaker behaves in front of an audience is crucial. They are, after all, in the spotlight, and therefore, everything they do will be observed. It is also worth remembering that so is everyone else in the pitch team. Therefore, everybody has a responsibility for thinking about the way they act, and to be aware how their behavior can shape the customer's perception and influence the dynamic of the presentation, both positively and negatively.

What It Means to Own the Floor

The presenter is in the spotlight, and they own the floor. What this means is that the audience becomes subordinate. They have handed control of the meeting to the presenter who not only owns the content but also controls the physical space. It is for the presenter to choose how they engage the audience, communicate the story, and drive key messages home.

How the presenter uses the physical space depends on how the meeting is set up. Remember, pitching is quite different to public speaking, where someone is speaking to an audience in an auditorium. In a meeting room, there is obviously a lot less space and the focus will be on either documents or handouts brought to the meeting, or a presentation via a screen on the wall. However, there is often some space to move.

Standing up gives the speaker a big advantage, even in a relatively small room. Clearly, if everyone else is seated, they dominate the room. This means they can be seen and heard by everyone, and just as importantly, they can see the faces of every customer.

Making sure everyone is engaged with and listening to a presentation is much easier to do standing up. All the speaker has to do is look directly at someone in the audience, and inevitably they will grab the person's attention. As much as it is a way of getting attention, it is also a way of engaging everyone, because the speaker can ensure they talk to every customer in turn, which is a much more inclusive behavior.

Personal Insight

One of the key messages I always try to get across when running presentation skills training is that being a presenter is not the same as being an actor. In a way, it is hard to blame anyone for jumping to this conclusion given the number of training courses that have advocated a presentation method. Suggestions that include standing with feet apart, hands by one's side, and similar ideas amuse me for two reasons. One is that they seem so artificial. The idea that there is a way of presenting that is set in stone seems so counterintuitive. Just look at the TED talk and see how different they are. The other point is where I watch people try to apply these rules, to the point where the presentation ceases to be about communicating at all. Far from representing business, I had been transported back to university and was looking at a class about method acting! People should present in their own skin. This doesn't mean they can't learn how to speak in public or at a meeting with a customer. What is important is that they behave authentically, and don't think they have to pretend to be something they're not. Apart from the obvious difficulty in getting people to learn rigid presentation rules, there is an important business reason for not doing so. Business presentations are often, and accurately, described as chemistry meetings. The idea is that they are a test of whether the customer and the supplier get on and will be able to work together effectively. Given that business relationships sometimes mean people spend more time with their customers or suppliers than they do with their partners, it is important both parties get on. Therefore, from a pitch perspective, it is really important the supplier's pitch team behave the way they normally do. The customer is buying products, services, and solutions from a supplier who employs people, and therefore, there is no value turning up to a pitch "in character," instead of yourself. The mantra I espouse is to always present in your own skin.

Movement

There is nothing wrong with presenting standing still, but there are sometimes benefits from movement. For example, moving toward the screen allows the presenter to emphasize a key point, or to explain a diagram, or to underline a key message.

The act of moving itself will lead to short pauses in a presentation, which is good because it gives everyone a moment to think. It also creates energy because the speaker appears more expressive.

Hand Gestures

Hands are expressive too. They communicate and reinforce what is being said. Using hand gestures is a perfectly normal thing to do and can help a speaker underline a key message. For example, counting out a number of features of a product creates emphasis and creates time for the audience to take in the benefit.

Other gestures include using a sweeping hand to represent the inclusion of the wider audience or the team in what is being discussed. Opening hands toward an audience meaning "you" and closing the fingers back onto the palms meaning "us" to emphasize or underline working together.

The point of listing these nonverbal communicators is not to suggest that there is a list of good gestures or hand-movements a speaker needs to learn. It is instead to point out the obvious thing that when people talk to each other, they naturally use hand gestures to express themselves, and that the presenter should feel they can use them too if it helps them to engage the audience and to communicate and underline what they are saying. It also makes a speaker appear more natural and more authentic.

Props

The obvious prop that will most likely be used, and one that has already been mentioned, is the presentation that runs on a projector or a screen. Using a screen is a perfectly acceptable way to present; however, it can become overbearing. The "death by PowerPoint" experience is something everyone will know, quite possibly from both sides of the meeting table! Just because a presentation is long, doesn't mean it has to be insufferable. However, if everything is being presented from a screen, then inevitably it can become monotonous, over time. This is where props come in.

A prop is literally anything that becomes the focus of discussion away from the screen, including a demonstration product or sample, or a document, flowchart, or diagram. The point of a prop, in the context of communication, is to disrupt the meeting by taking everyone's attention off the screen and bring it back to the presenter and the pitch team.

A prop allows interaction with the customer in a direct way that wouldn't happen when the audience is focused on a screen. For example, a pitch team might present a flow chart of one of the processes they run to deliver specific services to the customer. Printing it out makes it visual. Putting it onto the table and taking the customer through it step-by-step using the diagram makes it easier to understand and is likely to prompt questions and more discussion.

The prop, because it is physical, is also something that can be left behind at the end of a meeting—a tangible reminder of what was talked about.

How to Engage an Audience Around the Meeting Table

Standing up and moving about is probably the best way to engage an audience. However, that isn't always practical, and after all, it is the customer who decides the format of the meeting.

If a meeting is setup with everyone sitting around a table, that doesn't mean the presentation team cannot properly engage with the customer. However, there are few specific challenges they may need to overcome.

If there are several people representing the supplier siting side by side, then the first obvious problem is that those sitting on either end of the line cannot see each other. Therefore, they cannot interact in the way they would have done, if the speaker had been standing up.

It is possible to avoid the presentation team having to crane necks to see each other, if the line is slightly curved. For example, if the pitch team in the middle move their chairs back a little bit. Team members at each end will be able to see each other, as well as those in the middle of the line.

In terms of engagement, just as with the stand-up presenter, it is important the speaker is working the room and engaging directly with each member of the audience. Having sat on the customer's side, it is extremely off-putting if a presenter only speaks to one member of the audience. In any normal setting, this would never happen because it would be considered rude.

Distractions

One of the manifestations of being nervous is for a speaker to develop presentation tics. Away from presentations, tics are real and serious things. They are unwanted, involuntary, and repetitive movements of parts of the body (motor tics) or involuntary sounds (vocal tics). Presentation tics are temporary and are driven by fear and stress. They manifest themselves in a number of ways including swaying from side to side, dancing feet (stepping weight from one foot to the other repeatedly), tapping fingers, jingling change, or something else in the pocket, repeatedly clearing the throat, or adding other emphatic interjections such as "erm," "umm," or "err" at the beginning of every sentence.

Such behaviors are often unnoticed by the person. They are, however, distracting to the audience. The way to deal with these distractions is through practice and rehearsal.

Engagement (or Lack of)

One of the curious things about presentation teams is how often they are active participants only when it's their turn to be in the spotlight, that is, when they are speaking and not when other team members are speaking. It's almost as though they spark into life from standby mode to speak, only to switch off afterward.

Every team member will have listened to one of their team speak before, and if they have engaged in becoming a Master of Persuasion should know the Story Plan inside out. However, that is no excuse to switch off. The job of all nonspeakers is to be active listeners in front of the customer. After all, why should a customer be interested in what a supplier is talking about if everyone else in their pitch team isn't paying attention?

What is worse is if the rest of the team actively distract the audience from what the speaker is saying, even if they do so accidentally. Distraction activities are many and various, but include popping the end of a pen, or twirling it round in the fingers, looking out of the window or up at the ceiling, doodling on a piece of paper, or whispering to other colleagues. All these activities distract attention from the speaker.

The job of the nonspeaking team is to be fully engaged with what is being said, to be supportive of the speaker so that the impression the wider pitch team convey collectively, is that what their colleague is talking about is important and relevant to the customer; and worth listening to. Distractions inevitably create the impression that what is being said doesn't matter.

How to Control and Project the Voice

The voice is a powerful instrument. Although business presentations are dry by comparison to the performance of an actor in a play or film, that shouldn't mean the capabilities of the voice should be ignored when communicating with a customer.

When we listen to someone who speaks well, we hear a richness in their voice that demands our attention, stimulates us to think, and stirs our emotions on many different levels.

Speaking is something everyone takes for granted, and in a normal setting, most people would not think carefully about whether they should modify how they speak; and that is because modifying the voice is something everyone does naturally without thinking.

Pitching is not a normal situation nor done in a normal setting. However, how someone projects their voice will have an impact on whether a presentation is successful and whether it is convincing and persuasive to a customer.

A number of aspects of speaking can make a difference to how a presenter sounds, including rhythm, intonation, and inflection.

Rhythm in Speech

From a high-level perspective, rhythm is the sense of movement in terms of the timing, stress, and number of syllables in speech. It has an impact on whether the listener understands what someone is saying.

English is a rhythmic language, with a regular pattern of stressed and unstressed syllables. The rhythm of English is different to other languages, which is why sometimes it can be harder to understand a non-native speaker, speak English, because their natural speech rhythm is different.

The rhythm of speech is affected by the speed at which someone is speaking. When it comes to presenting, a common problem is that people get nervous and talk too quickly.

From a speech perspective, the consequence of speaking too quickly is that vowels and consonants, that should be distinct, begin to sound like each other (assimilation), and sounds or syllables can be omitted completely, which results in words being shortened (e.g., He is to he's) (elision). The point about these very common effects on language is that they do not make it easier for an audience. The reverse is true, because the speaker will inevitably be talking much faster, and the audience will have to try harder to listen to and process all this information much faster too.

The remedy is to slow down. Not to speak slowly, but to be measured in terms of the pace of speaking. Some suggest speakers practice using a metronome to establish a rhythm that gives them the time they need to speak clearly. The audience needs to be able to follow what someone is saying easily. If they can't hear it, they can't understand it and therefore cannot be persuaded by it either.

Intonation

Intonation is the rise and fall of the pitch of the voice and is associated with the emotions being expressed by a speaker. It is often described as the music of the voice.

In the context of pitching for business, raising and lowering the pitch of a voice enables a speaker to communicate their excitement, interest, and enthusiasm for what they are talking about. Being positive and enthusiastic, without going over the top, is important. If the supplier cannot display enthusiasm and commitment for their own proposal, then who can?

The effect on the listener is really positive, because it makes the speaker much more interesting to listen to, than say a presentation delivered with a monotone voice. It is through expressing this energy and commitment that the speaker becomes significantly more persuasive.

Intonation is a feature of everyday speaking. It isn't something that only happens in speeches or at presentations. Therefore, it is something everyone uses every day, and with a bit of conscious thought and practice can enhance the impact of a presenter very significantly.

Inflection

Inflection is the way a speaker emphasizes a particular part of a word to add weight and meaning to it. In this way, a speaker can underline something they want the audience to recognize is important.

For example, imagine saying the following sentence: "The reason we have proposed product X is because it is the best solution." Clearly, it can be read exactly as it is written, with every word being given the same stress.

However, it also possible to add emphasis in two ways that change how the same sentence will be heard and understood by the audience.

(a) The **reason** we have proposed product X is because it is the **best** solution.

(b) The reason we have **proposed** product X is because it **is** the best solution.

In example (a), the words "reason" and "best" are stressed. This is intended to sound sincere and underline the message that the solution is the "best" in the mind of the customer.

In example (b), the words "proposed" and "is" are stressed. This is a more assertive way of speaking, which underlines a confidence in what has been proposed.

Inflection is a really useful thing to learn, which can really change the impact on the customer. Clearly, time allowing, what should be stressed could be a key point of discussion in a final rehearsal.

Dramatic Pause

A pause is a deliberate short gap between sentences. The pause has a number of purposes and is a versatile tool in terms of public speaking and presenting. Apart from providing an opportunity to take a breath, it breaks a presentation up. It provides a moment of time for the audience to absorb and think about what they have been told, and it is also a moment for the presenter to reset themselves ready to move on to the next point.

Pauses are also useful in indicating a change in direction of the presentation. For example, if a presentation is in sections or has a number of discreet topics, then it is natural to pause for a few seconds when the speaker has finished one section or point before moving onto the next. This helps the audience to follow the story.

Both of these examples reflect what happens in normal speech, and it is sometimes worthwhile for a presenter to remember to include pauses in the way they deliver a presentation, as it makes it so much easier for the listener to follow what is being said. Thinking about pausing is also useful in helping to identify when sentences are too long.

The idea of a dramatic pause is where a pause is used not only to break sentences or parts of a presentation up but to demand the audience's attention. The construct is a simple one. The speaker might ask a rhetorical question or make an assertion, or claim, and pause for several seconds before answering their own question or explaining the assertion.

For example, imagine the speaker says, "I am now going to explain the reasons our solution will transform your business" **<Dramatic Pause>** "First, . . ."

The dramatic pause demands the full undivided attention of the audience. It signals to them that something important or significant is going to be said. It is, therefore, a very useful way of referencing benefits and key messages, and works really well provided it is not overused.

Rule of Three

This rule has its origins in Roman times and is a speech mechanism that has been used for years by many speakers, including famous politicians and broadcasters.

The idea is a simple one. In constructing a speech, there should be three points in support of an assertion, proposition, or message, as this is deemed the most effective way of communicating with an audience.

Three is the magic number because people remember three connected points, whereas they won't remember a much longer list. Having three points that support an assertion or argument lends it a sense of power and credibility, that is, therefore sometimes more convincing and persuasive. In terms of listening, having three points simply sounds more pleasant.

An entire presentation cannot always be written using the Rule of Three. However, it is certainly very applicable when summarizing the benefits or key features of a proposal, to wrap up a specific section or in the concluding remarks at the end.

Signposting

Signposting is a technique to make sure the audience clearly understand what they have been told, and a way of providing them with context about what is going to be spoken about next.

For example, imagine a presentation has several sections covering a number of different topics. Before beginning a section, the speaker sets out in simple terms what they will be talking about. Then, at the end, they recap what they have just been speaking about, before repeating the exercise for the next section.

The value of this approach is two-fold. Firstly, it provides the speaker with an opportunity to communicate key messages. For example, the speaker could introduce a section by saying they intend to cover the most important features of the proposed solution and explain how they will add value to the customer's business. Straightaway, the audience knows the context of the next section and is also primed to listen to the features. Then, at the end of the section, signposting provides the speaker with the opportunity to recap, to summarize what those key benefits are before moving on. This, in communication terms, provides two bites of the cherry to persuade the customer.

The second benefit is to facilitate a presentation that has multiple speakers, because signposting allows for a coherent handover from one speaker to the next. Speaker 1 can introduce Speaker 2 and summarize the topic they will be covering. Bearing in mind that the audience won't know the Story Plan, it provides structure and context for the audience, and that means they already have the right mindset to be active listeners the moment the next person begins speaking.

Personal Insight

There were few occasions when at the start of a presentation skills workshop, one of the participants wouldn't openly admit that they were scared of presenting or terrible at doing it, or both! It was almost like people would get their excuses in first, especially when they saw the video camera had been set up. If presenting wasn't something they naturally enjoyed, then being filmed made it ten times worse. The purpose of teaching presentations skills is not to humiliate or scare anyone. In my view, the more someone comes to understand how presenting works (as a discipline) the easier it gets. It's actually in some ways more important to debunk what many people think presenting is all about. The purpose of using a camera to record someone presenting was for two reasons. The first was it brought a heightened degree of pressure to the session, which created a setting that was as near as possible to the real deal of presenting to a customer. From a practical perspective, filming the presentation allowed me to playback what the presenter did, because it would be impossible to remember what someone said verbatim. What was almost always true was that a person's opinion of themselves, of their ability to present, was always much worse than it actually was. People would say they felt nervous and were shaking, and couldn't think clearly, and therefore muddled up what they were saying, and they were unable to speak clearly, and so on. Comparing the personal criticism to the film almost always showed how very little came across. From the outside, they looked and sounded fine. What was actually going wrong was that they couldn't remember what they were supposed to be saying. That was the stumbling block, more than their ability to present. The stress of the moment was the cause of their lack of confidence, and this is relatively easy to solve with practice.

Presentation Practicalities

Why Process Is a Safety Net for Nervous Speakers

For less confident speakers, this process provides an important and useful safety net. Many people think of presenting or public speaking as an exercise rooted in thinking on one's feet, in having the capability to make things up on the spur of the movement with ease.

For nervous speakers, this image presents a nightmare scenario because the act of delivering a speech is nerve wracking and challenging enough. Nerves manifest themselves in a number of ways, a dry mouth, palpitations, blanking out, or losing the thread of what was being said, or conversely, speakers find themselves infused with a sudden burst of adrenaline and burst into life and speak at a thousand miles an hour!

This process advocates carefully planning pitches rather than jumping into delivering them off the cuff. Great communication is the result of a Communication Objective, a Meeting Goal, a clear Story Plan, carefully selected Content, and thought being put into Style and Language. All this happens before presenting to the customer begins.

What makes the process a safety net for those who find delivering presentations challenging is that it is a comprehensive and detailed blueprint of what needs to be presented. It provides the intellectual reasoning as to why communicating this story is the right thing to do. Slides, or other meeting props, are created from this thinking. Everyone involved in the presentation will be familiar with the same blueprint, and therefore, because there is a Story Plan, presenting (individually and as a team) is something that can be rehearsed and practiced. The whole process, therefore, makes presenting easier (if not easy!).

Referring to Notes or a Script When Presenting

Some people have a strong opinion that presentations ought to be presented note and script-free. The view is that the act of referencing notes undermines the impact of a presentation and the presence of the speaker. It is deemed to signal that the speaker lacks confidence either in themselves or in the content they are presenting.

Referencing a script is certainly problematic. It is true that if a speaker is reading a statement out loud from a script, then the attitude and atmosphere at a presentation can be adversely affected, and what makes this really apparent is the sentiment of what is being said.

Imagine a meeting where the speaker is reading from a script when describing how the supplier is committed to providing outstanding service to the customer. The script, because it is prepared in advance, undermines the statement of commitment; after all, why would the presenter not be able to express this feeling themselves?

The other obvious problem using a script is when the speaker loses their place, and therefore has to stop speaking to locate where they are. This clearly makes things difficult, and really ought to be avoided.

Those who feel the need to read from a script are likely to be under-prepared and under rehearsed in terms of giving presentations. Having a script is an obvious mental crutch, as the person doesn't have to remember the content they are speaking about. However, it is highly likely that if the person is taken out of the meeting or presentation setting, they will be more than capable of explaining the content. It is the situation that is the problem, not the ability of the speaker.

Presenting is something that everyone can get better at, even nervous speakers. The way to get better is to practice speaking out loud and to rehearse presenting the content they intend to present live in a presentation. This is the only way to become a more confident and better speaker.

Speaker notes (or cue-cards) are quite different from a script, and there is no reason why a speaker shouldn't have a set of bullet points to remind them what they should be talking about. Not everyone needs them, but it is clearly much better to have them than to miss key points.

How Detailed Should Slides Be?

There is always a lot of debate about whether there is a standard in terms of the amount of content a slide should contain. The point made earlier is that slides are an opportunity to communicate directly with an audience. Therefore, the information they present and the messages they communicate are important. The audience will be focused on a presenter, but they also will read the slides at the same time.

Slides that are essentially speaker notes or cue-cards are pointless, in that they add nothing to the meeting other than to signal the list of topics that will be spoken about. It, therefore, makes sense to have slides that have a communication purpose and that explain something of value to the customer or reinforce key messages.

This does not exclude slides that carry a lot of detail, whether in the form of a diagram or text. However, briefly referencing a slide that contains a lot detail before moving rapidly on to the next does not aid communication. Therefore, if the presentation doesn't allow time to cover a slide properly, then it is good practice to omit the slide rather than to present it and immediately gloss over it. If the detail is worth going into, then the rest of the presentation should be edited to fit the available time.

Rehearsing

How many people would pick up a tennis racket for the first time, play a game, and expect to be really good? Maybe some people do this, but they are rare. As it is with most things, skills have to be learned properly and perfected through practice, and the skill of presenting is no different.

Imagine going to a theater performance. Everyone would recognize that there are two things that need to be done well. The first being the focus on an actor, who needs to perform well individually. The second being a focus on the cast as a whole, who all need to perform well together. When both parts work well, the performance works well. When an individual or the collective doesn't perform well, then the impact and enjoyment overall is diminished.

Presenting, in many ways, is similar to a stage performance. Individuals need to perform well, but so also does the pitch team, which is why businesses should focus on the "performance" as well the presentation content, and recognize everyone plays their part, whenever they are speaking but also when they are not; and to do it well requires practice and rehearsal.

Practice Makes Perfect

Practice makes perfect is so true of presenting. The more someone presents, the better they get at doing it. However, it probably isn't wise to practice on customers. In fact, given the amount of time and effort that is invested in winning business, it seems extraordinarily negligent not to learn and practice presentation skills, and instead leave performance to the gods.

If the pitch to a customer is the first time a presenter speaks something out loud, then, by definition, they have not rehearsed or practiced at all. Just as in the example of tennis, applied to presenting, who would expect this approach to deliver the best and most persuasive result?

It is, therefore, important for individuals to practice out loud. They need to rehearse how they will talk through the topics they are to cover, so they become familiar with speaking about them. They also need to hear how they sound, to assess whether what they are saying makes sense and be certain they are getting across the key points they want to communicate to the customer.

Because every smartphone has a camera, it is possible for virtually everyone to record themselves practicing, so a speaker can play their presentation back, and keep practicing it until they are confident, they have got it right.

Team Rehearsal

As with the example of performing in a theater, being a good presenter individually is one aspect of a presentation. The pitch team as a whole also needs to work well together, and that comes from practice.

The more often the team pitch to customers together, the better they get, as a team. Of course, from a customer's perspective, the focus at a presentation will always be on the speaker. However, that does not mean the other pitch team members are irrelevant. The way they listen and behave will have a big impact on the audience too. The more they appear to be a team, demonstrating a confidence and familiarity of working together, the stronger the impression they will make on the customer.

Before the pitch takes place live, rehearsing as a team is a great way to polish and perfect the presentation. The pitch team should be supportive of each other, rather than appearing to be a bear pit. Every member of the team should feel able to provide constructive feedback to improve the impact of what is being said, to point out the parts that don't flow well, and to provide positive encouragement to less confident members of the team.

Rehearsal is also important because it confirms timings and helps a team to practice how one speaker will hand over to another, if different sections are being presented by different speakers. Clearly, if the speaker of a section of the presentation becomes familiar with what the preceding speaker is saying, then they will be ready to take up the role as presenter seamlessly when their times comes.

Personal Insight

Rehearsal is defined as a trial for a future public performance. However, it is quite common for pitch teams not to take the rehearsal seriously. It is as though "performing" in front of colleagues is harder and more embarrassing than presenting to a customer. One of the common mistakes in approaching rehearsal is to treat it as though it is a read through, each person describing what they intend to cover, instead of delivering it as though for real. As a consultant to pitch teams in all sort of industries, I try to encourage suppliers not to do this, as a read through is a bit of waste of time for a number of reasons. The content isn't close to what will actually be said, and it doesn't reveal is how long it will take for each speaker to deliver their bit. As I am not involved in the final presentation to the customer, I always ask for feedback. How did it go? One of the common responses is that the presentation didn't go exactly to plan because the amount of time allocated to each speaker turned out to be unrealistic. In other words, the pitch team ran out of time, and therefore had to rush or cut the last few sections of the presentation. Estimating timings isn't easy to do from what is written on a slide, because how long it takes depends on how the person presents it, on what they say, and how they embellish the points they want to make. The very act of presenting can provoke verbosity and people lose track of time, in the thick of it. Every minute a presenter speaks longer than was intended equals a minute that will have to be deducted from someone else's slot. This quite common experience really underlines why rehearsing properly is so beneficial and should be a regular activity for all pitch teams.

The Dry Run

The step above a normal rehearsal is often termed a dry run, where the supplier attempts to create as closely as possible the conditions that mimic the real-world experience the pitch team will face in front of the customer.

This is a good idea, because creating a degree of tension and pressure is good practice for the real event, and if the audience, of handpicked colleagues, plays their part properly, is a much better test of not only their performance of the pitch team but also whether the content and structure works as well as it was hoped it would.

As well as observing the presentation as though "live," the audience can also prepare questions to test the pitch team on topics or points that are deemed the hardest to answer, in anticipation these may well be ones that come up. Finally, it is also a great way to check whether the timings allocated to each section are correct, and therefore, whether the Story Plan needs to be modified or the speaker needs to change their approach and cut out some things.

Personal Insight

Filming the rehearsal or the dry run is really instructive, because it clearly shows the pitch team exactly how they sound and look, and it also provides the opportunity to assess content in detail. It is also extremely useful to see how the pitch team interact with each other, and to test whether they act as a team, which is what they should do. Being an outsider can be a big help in a rehearsal, because it is easier to see what's wrong and provide detailed constructive criticism. Although a consultant has been hired by someone at the supplier, they don't have the same relationships with senior management, which sometimes allows me to say things everyone is thinking but others, who are more junior, simply don't think they can say. The behavior of the pitch team as a whole, and in particular the senior manager, was a real problem with one client I worked with. Fortunately, I had filmed the dry run and had time to play back a 20-minute presentation. The content on the whole was good, but the interaction was extremely poor as nearly everyone spent the time they weren't speaking, doing a great job of distracting the audience. This included twirling a pen, looking out of the window, and doodling on a pad, and the person who was probably the worst culprit was the senior manager of the team, who had a habit of tapping their pen on the table. The film was irrefutable, and therefore something that was easy to point out, and everyone could see exactly how dysfunctional it made them appear as a team. It also allowed me to challenge their collective attitude. One of the key messages they wanted to communicate was the level and quality of the service the customer would receive. They talked about how the customer service team would work together to address problems quickly. My challenge to them was whether they thought that message was helped or hindered by the lack of respect they showed team members when they were speaking? Did they think they acted as a team? Did they think the customer would look at them and feel reassured they would receive the kind of service they wanted from this group of people? The obvious answer was no. It is all well and good for the supplier to have principles and values that shape the way they work, that they were proud of, but it is equally as important these principles are evident to the customer whenever they interact with the supplier. Therefore, the behavior of the supplier has to live up to the commitments they have made, or these commitments will appear hollow.

What's Different About Presenting Online

The global pandemic clearly had a significant impact on business through-out the world, resulting in people working from home, and business being conducted online. The number of face-to-face meetings has significantly decreased, even after governments relaxed restrictions with regard to personal movement. Many companies have chosen to keep their staff working from home, and essential travel has been redefined.

Meetings have moved online, and the major software companies, and some new players, offer platforms to host meetings of all sizes, including sales pitches and presentations.

However, meeting a customer online is quite different to meeting them face-to-face because it requires, if not a completely different approach, a new way of talking and presenting, additional planning, and careful management.

While every point already covered in this chapter applies to presentations and customer meetings online as it does to pitches and presentations that are face-to-face, a number of specific considerations can help ensure online conference and video calls are successful.

Conference and Video Call Management

Online video conferencing technology works best person to person, or with a small group. When two people meet online it really isn't different to them meeting in person. However, as soon as the meeting group expands, and especially when it involves customers as well as suppliers, then everything becomes significantly harder to manage.

The worst kind of call is one which turns into a free for all, where speakers interject and interrupt each other. If it were a piece of music, the worst conference call would be described as staccato, where each note (or voice in this case) is detached and separated from all the others.

One of the reasons it is difficult to manage conference calls, compared to face-to-face meetings, is, in part, because of the way the technology works. Video conferencing technology responds to the active voice and switches the face that appears in the main window to whomever is speaking automatically.

Therefore, as soon as anyone on the call starts talking or even when they make an audible and distinctive sound, the video conferencing software will automatically replace the person currently active and whose face is displayed in the main screen, with the person who has started speaking (or is the source of the noise). As soon as this happens, it is a natural reflex action for the current active speaker to stop talking.

This is why conference call golden rule number 1 is to always be on mute, until it's your turn to speak. However, people forget, and those who have braved (or valiantly embraced) the new world of work that has become dominated by conference and video calls will have learned this!

Of course, disruption, when participants interject or interrupt someone who is speaking, is not always intentional. In fact, the cause is often due to the way we naturally converse. We talk all the time, and when we talk to others, meaning when we have a conversation, we follow a set of rules that we have learned from childhood that are the antithesis of conference and video call best practice.

The flow of a conversation, the back and forth, is really what makes conversations fun. Clarifying what someone means by asking a question, or commenting on something someone has said is perfectly normal. When people don't follow the rules of conversation, things can actually become rather awkward. It starts to feel like you are talking in a vacuum, which is quite strange.

Interjecting with supportive remarks and phatic responses are another good example of standard conversational behavior. In a conversation that takes place across a table, or even at a customer presentation, when someone makes a good point it would be perfectly normal for someone to interject in a supportive or confirmatory way. They might say "Good Point" or "Yes" or other words that express their agreement or support.

Imagine what happens when these perfectly normal behaviors are transferred to a video conference call? Whoever is speaking is likely to stop in their tracks. The flow of what they were talking about will be lost, and there will then have to be a conversation to clarify the interrupter doesn't want to speak before the original speaker carries on.

The lack of conversation, of the back and forth we are all used to, is challenging for everyone, because whomever is speaking has to be focused. They need to say what they need to say, without any of the normal conversational injections, and this requires a lot more concentration. It also requires them to be absolutely clear what they are talking about.

This is where the Story Plan comes into its own, especially where a call involves the customer. The Story Plan contains a list of topics and details that will be covered, set out in a logical and meaningful sequence. Therefore, it is a blueprint everyone can use to help them to manage the call.

Managing the Flow of a Presentation to a Customer

The smoothest presentations flow seamlessly. Even when a person finishes their part, and hands over to someone else, there is no stalling or significant pauses before the next person starts to speak.

This is best practice because once there is a delay between speakers, the listener may lose their train of thought. The energy is somehow lost, and the speaker will then have to work doubly hard to get everyone's attention back.

The virtual team, of course, cannot see each other in the same way they would be able to in a physical meeting. They will, of course, see the faces of their colleagues. However, it is much harder for team members to communicate with each other, and that is what makes it harder to achieve a seamless flow throughout a presentation on a conference or video call.

Managing a presentation or a pitch seamlessly requires more than a Story Plan. The Story Plan explains topics that will be covered in reasonable detail, but not enough detail so everyone knows precisely when a section will end, and it's their turn to speak.

Therefore, the team has two choices. They either determine exactly how they will finish their part, and let the next speaker know so they are listening out for their cue to come in, or the current speaker uses the Signposting technique, summarizes what they have been talking about, and introduces the next speaker who will, therefore, be ready to pick things up immediately.

Managing Body Language on a Conference Call

Active listening, where you make clear to the speaker and everyone else on the video call how interested you are in what is being said, is the modus operandi for every member of a pitch team. For obvious reasons, anything but complete concentration on what is being said will be a distraction.

Where there are a number of people on a call, it is common to view in gallery-mode, so everyone can be seen. Because of the position of the camera, the face will be in close up inside a frame. Every facial expression and every movement will be seen immediately by everyone.

However, being completely focused every second is what is required from every pitch team member, and there is no doubt this is hard work especially if the participant has to spend most of the call waiting for their turn to speak or perhaps are only attending to answer the odd question at the end.

Inevitably, people become distracted and forget they are on view. They move about, talk to other people who have come into the room where they are taking the call, leave their desk to get a drink, take calls on their mobile phones, write e-mails, and so on.

Of course, all these activities would never happen face-to-face. No one would dream of doing anything like it if they were sitting in the same room as the customer. Imagine being in the middle of a pitch, and suddenly one of the team pulls out a phone and takes a call, or gets up and walks out?

Hard though it is, there are a couple of things the supplier can do to focus the pitch team on what is required. The first step is to make sure the pitch team have a check list of things to do to prepare for an important customer presentation or pitch. This should include having a clear and tidy space wherever they are taking the video conference call. Everything the participant needs should be ready, including pens, paper, drinks, and any files or paperwork they need to refer to. It might even be better to have some documents printed out, so the participant doesn't need to go searching through e-mails or folders to find those documents that are most likely to need to reference. Home deliveries should be planned so they don't interrupt the call, and finally, but not least, everyone in the pitch team should make sure they don't need a comfort break in the middle of the call!

All of this is really standard preparation and would be automatic if the supplier was going to the customer's offices to meet them. Being remote somehow brings with it a lot of lax behavior, which is entirely avoidable, with a little thought. However, even if all of this preparation is followed to a T, it is hard to look interested on video conference calls for extended periods of time.

One option that can be considered if for each member of the team to upload their personal photo to the video conference software and add it to their profile. When video is enabled on a call, everyone will see them "live." However, if a participant turns video off, the profile picture will be displayed instead.

Then, when the participant wants to contribute something or it is their turn to present, they activate video, and the profile picture will be replaced by the live shot of them instead. This approach, therefore, avoids the things people do wrong, however inadvertently. This approach does require everyone to remain attentive throughout, so they are ready to come in if asked, and it is also a good idea to inform the customer how the pitch team intend to manage the call, because it is possible the customer might think the supplier's pitch team are acting strangely, if everyone switches their video off.

Managing Questions and Answers Online

Conversations break presenting online norms, where a speaker might expect to be able to talk without interruption. In a conversation, it is normal to stop someone in mid-sentence and ask them to clarify or confirm something.

However, from a supplier's perspective who is pitching or presenting to a customer online, being interrupted is the last thing they would want to happen, because once the meeting has moved into a question-and-answer format, they may never get to finish their presentation, and they will have completely lost control of the agenda.

The fact people cannot be seen properly in a virtual room makes it extremely difficult to manage them, even if an attempt has been made to agree the rules for handling questions and answers with the customer beforehand, as even with agreement sometimes things go wrong. So, the supplier needs to have a Plan B.

The best way for the supplier to manage questions that disrupt their pitch or presentation is to have someone in the team to be the co-ordinator, like a maître d'hôtel, whose job is to handle any questions or interruptions from the customer.

Having a co-ordinator is a very effective way of handling things. To begin with, the rest of the supplier's pitch team know they are to wait for the co-ordinator to decide how to respond to a question rather than jump straight in to answering it.

Secondly, the co-ordinator can manage the situation, to perhaps put answering questions off until the team has finished their presentation. Or, if that isn't possible, they can filter questions. For example, if the customer were to ask a quite broad question, they can break the question down into a number of points, and then ask different members of the team to answer each part, in turn.

Of course, questions are asked not only by customers but also by suppliers. It, therefore, makes a lot of sense to plan questions before the meeting and agree how best to ask them. The same co-ordinator approach may be the best solution, or the team might have a preference for a different approach. The point is that it is much harder to wing a meeting online; in the way, it is possible when everyone is in the same room together. Therefore, the onus is on the supplier's pitch team to agree on a plan in advance.

Chat

Video conference software often has a chat feature, which can be used by attendees to post comments to everyone on the conference or video call or send a private message to a specific individual.

In many ways, Chat provides the opportunity for the supplier's pitch or presentation team to communicate in a way they wouldn't be able to in a physical meeting space. However, it is best planned in advance, to ensure the presentation team know to actively use Chat and have it enabled (otherwise they may not see messages that are sent).

Chat can be useful for a number of things. For example, if the team see that the responses of the customer indicate things aren't going well, the team or current presenter has the opportunity to change the approach or move on to the next topic. One member of the presentation team can be the timekeeper and manage Chat to keep everything running to the agreed schedule. It can also be used to proactively handle customer questions and in more general terms allows members of the team to post ideas and thoughts to everyone else.

If the video meeting software being used doesn't allow this, then running chat software separately is an alternative.

Lip-Reading

One of the obvious differences between face-to-face meets and video conference calls is that the individual participant chooses how they will appear on screen at a conference call.

This choice is largely driven by technology and how the individual hosts the conference call. If the participant is using a built-in laptop camera, they are only able to control the angle of the screen and how far they sit away from it. If the camera is independent to the computer, there is a lot more flexibility.

Why does this matter? One of the things people frequently do when listening to other people speak is to watch their lips as well as listen to what they are saying. This isn't only something done by people who are hard of hearing, but also by others for a number of reasons. There may be ambient sound making it harder for them to hear. English may not be their first language, and therefore, reading lips helps them to comprehend what is being said more easily.

Therefore, it is worthwhile for every participant to think about how they are appearing, and whether the position of the camera and where they sit in relation to it hinders or enables other participants to lip read.

Pronunciation and Clear Speaking

Listening to someone speak requires good concentration and bearing in mind the purpose of the meeting from the supplier's perspective is to communicate and persuade a customer to buy from them, it is even more important that the presentation team does everything it can to make it as easy as possible for the listener.

The technology, however good it is, can sometimes distort the voice or adds noise. Therefore, speakers need to be much more aware of the need to speak clearly and slowly, and to pronounce words crisply, so they can be certain the audience will hear them.

Personal Appearance and Setting

No one would argue that personal appearance does not matter in business. In terms of clothes, clearly what constitutes appropriate wear depends on the situation, and may also be driven by the industry or business sector an individual works in, as there may be expectations to meet. How an individual looks is important, and so is the setting in which the call is made.

The important point is to remember that in terms of winning work, how someone appears will influence and shape the perception of a customer. Even though it is possible to be critical of someone who makes a superficial judgment about someone, based primarily on their appearance or their home (if that is where the call is made), it is also worth remembering that a new customer doesn't have a knowledge of the supplier or a relationship with them. Therefore, how they appear is one point of reference in helping the customer make up their mind about who to choose to work with.

Personal appearance matters as much on a video conference call as it does at a physical meeting. It is a big mistake to think that just because the call is made from home, rather than an office meeting room, that it doesn't matter how a person looks and it won't influence the customer.

There are two important goals, from a supplier's perspective, the first is to communicate a sense of professionalism and the second to avoid creating the wrong impression. Therefore, changes in working practices don't mean the supplier should dress or behave casually.

This requirement also extends to the setting of the place the conference call is made. Ideally whatever the setup technically, the participant won't need to wear headphones.

If the call is made from home, it is important to manage what is revealed in the room that will be visible to everyone else on the call. A view behind a participant that is cluttered and untidy probably won't project the best image to a customer, and it obviously makes sense not to have anything on view that the individual wouldn't want anyone to see.

Video Conference Technology

One of the obvious points about video conferencing is that the quality of the picture and sound is really important. The better they are the better it is.

Three things that determine conference quality include broadband connection speed and bandwidth, the camera and microphone, and lighting.

Clearly, even a fast broadband connection may not always be reliable, and that creates its own problems in terms of managing a call when things go wrong. However, the blunt truth is that the broadband service itself has to be up to business standards, and it isn't OK if the picture and sound quality are consistently poor.

The camera and microphone also need to be high quality. Laptops often have their own cameras and microphones built it, and some are not really great quality. The other point to remember is that if the camera is in the case of the laptop, there will be very little flexibility as to how the participant appears on screen. They will have to sit directly in front of the laptop in order to be seen and also to see any documents that might be shared or presented. Having a separate camera and microphone, therefore, may offer not only a better image and sound quality but also greater flexibility.

Lighting also needs to be considered. Firstly, it is important to be seen properly, and that can be made more difficult depending on the light fittings in the room. For example, if there is a bright light in the ceiling or bright sunshine through the window behind the caller, then it will make their face appear very dark by contrast and cast a halo-effect around their head. Therefore, the best light is that which illuminates the person, projected onto them as a whole from behind the camera. Some of the external cameras and microphones incorporate adjustable lights that illuminate the participant and compensate for poor lighting conditions.

CHAPTER 9

How to Use the Six-Step Process

How to Become a Master of Persuasion is a process to transform the communication capabilities of all suppliers and can be used for every pitch opportunity, big or small. There are three parts of the process, strategy, story, and delivery, and six steps that explain how a supplier's pitch team can prepare and plan how to persuade the customer they are the right supplier to choose.

Being persuasive has a formula, which is

$$\text{PROPOSITION} \times \text{POSITIONING} = \text{PERSUASION.}$$

Although the customer drives the sales process, the supplier will have numerous opportunities to persuade them that they are the best supplier to choose, provided they prepare properly and use each opportunity to its fullest extent.

Each part of the process is important in persuading the customer to select a supplier, which has been explained in the previous chapters of the book. The whole process is driven by 10 principles, which the supplier's pitch team should always remember, which are set out in the following (Figure 9.1).

The 10 Principles to Master the Art of Persuasion

1. Understand the Customer

Profiling the customer to learn about their world, and the issues and challenges they face, as well as a detailed analysis of their stated requirement, are the foundations of pitching. Responding to a customer's invitation to put forward a proposal without detailed understanding is unlikely to lead to success.

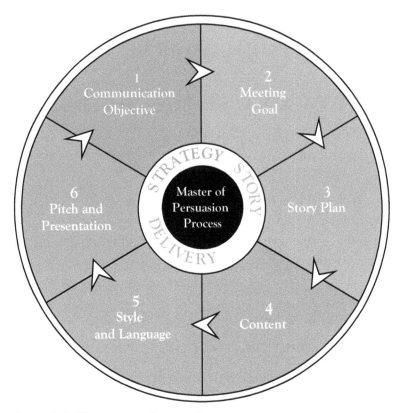

Figure 9.1 The process of persuasion

Applying the knowledge gained through analysis of Change Drivers and Customer Requirements enables the supplier to communicate more effectively with the customer as it enables the pitch team to focus on what is most important to them.

2. Take Every Opportunity to Pitch to the Customer

As with any relationship the more time both parties spend together, the more they get to know and understand each other. Every meeting or interaction with the customer will influence their choice of supplier. Each moment is a step in the sales process, and every moment presents the supplier with an opportunity to pitch to and persuade the customer they are the right supplier to choose.

3. Prepare for Each Meeting Occasion

Taking each meeting occasion seriously is the first step. However, it is not enough. The Meeting Goal is designed to focus the attention of the supplier's pitch team as to how they will take the relationship from the current to the future state by identifying what perceptions need to be challenged and what topics should be discussed.

From the supplier's perspective, every meeting should have a clear purpose, which helps the supplier move themselves further along the sales process, one step closer to winning.

4. Develop Business Stories That Flow Seamlessly

The business story is not a creative writing task, but one of assembling a Story Plan that covers the themes, topics, and specific details that will enable the supplier to deepen their relationship with the customer and to pitch and promote products, services, and solutions.

A story should flow seamlessly, from one topic to the next, in a way that is clear and obvious to the audience. It should also enable the supplier to communicate key messages.

5. Remember That Customers Are People

It is sometimes easy to forget that although businesses have processes and procure services from suppliers using ITTs and RFPs, they are run by people. People make the final decision, and they are no different to ordinary people and have prejudices, opinions, likes and dislikes, just as we all do.

When they read a proposal or listen to a presentation, the way they process information is conditioned by their opinion, judgment, and experience. They will be rational and emotional thinkers. So, it is vital the supplier considers who they will be writing for or presenting to and understands what will motivate them, so what they say is effective and persuasive.

6. Remember That Communication Is Only Effective When It Is Understood

One of the golden rules of communication is to be understood. Communication should always be meaningful and relevant, and meet the requirements of the Three Cs (concise, cohesive, and coherent) and the So What Test?

It should also be accessible and avoid jargon, business speak, and acronyms that obscure meaning and limit the impact of what is being communicated.

7. Believe in Yourself

If the supplier doesn't believe in itself, then who can? Therefore, communication needs to be assertive and leaves the customer in no doubt that the supplier believes in its proposal without hesitation, qualification, or doubt.

8. Make Sure What You Say and Write Matters

The supplier should be clear why what it proposes is the best solution for the customer. This means the positive reasons for choosing them should never be left for the customer to work out.

9. Remember That Everything You Do and Say In Front of an Audience Makes a Difference

Whenever supplier is in front of the customer, whether at a physical meeting or video conference call, what they say and the way they say it, the way they look, and how they behave will be observed and judged by the customer; and make a difference as to whether they are selected.

10. Practice Your Delivery

Delivery is not like acting. The customer wants authentic people who they can work with and whom they trust and value to help them. The act of delivery, speaking at a pitch meeting, is something that everyone can get better at doing, provided they prepare properly, practice, and rehearse.

About the Author

Tony Treacy has over 35 years' experience in business. He ran marketing director for a global firm, ran an award-winning agency working with some of the largest global brands, was a director at an international graphics business, and a specialist for a global company in the printing and publishing industry.

He set up his own company in 2010 and has been an independent consultant, a trainer, and coach since then, helping businesses to communicate their value and win new customers.

Tony is a fellow of the Marketing Society, an affiliate member of the Chartered Institute of Marketing, a mentor for the Business Growth Programme and managing director at Pitch Factory Limited, which is a member of the CPD Certification Service. *How to Become a Master of Persuasion* is based on two accredited CPD training courses: Storytelling and Pitching an Idea. Tony's company, Pitch Factory, run pitch training courses, and provides pitch coaching and pitch consultancy to business leaders and can be found at pitchfactory.com/

Index

ambition, 12
Ambition square, 14
aspirational sentiments, 82, 85–86
assertiveness, 74–75
audience, 99, 102

body language, 118–120

case study
    confectionary packaging industry
        supplier, 51–53
    implant office support services,
        48–49
    insurance services company, 56–58
    IT solution provider to the public
        sector, 49–51
    medical instrument manufacturer,
        45–47
    technology solutions provider to
        the finance sector, 53–55
Change Drivers, 6, 9–11, 20
    ambition, 12
    analysis, 13–16
    market, 11–12
    performance, 13
    regulation, 13
    worksheet, 14
chat, 121–122
clear speaking, 122–123
Communication Objective, 6, 9, 23
    Change Drivers (*See* Change
        Drivers)
    customer requirements, 16–19
    plan, 20–21, 46
    preparation, 19
    request for proposal, 21–22
    thinking, 10–11
Communication Objective Plan
    (COP), 20–21
conference, 116–118
content, 7, 59–60

emotional thinking, 63–66
rational thinking, 61–63, 65
So What Test, 68–70
Three Cs, 66–68
Content List, 36
contextual sentiments, 81, 83–84
customer
    current and future plans, 21–22
    flow seamlessly, 118
    knowledge, 27–28
    stakeholder, 60–65
    and supplier, 29–30
Customer Profile Change Drivers
    Worksheet, 14
Customer Profiling, 10–11, 19,
    23, 125
Customer Requirements, 11, 16–20

distractions, 103
dramatic pause, 106–107
dry run, 114
dysfunctional narratives, 68

emotional thinking, 63–66
engagement, 103–104
expositional sentiments, 82–83,
    87–89

financial performance, 13
flow seamlessly, 118

hand gestures, 101

impression, 3, 104, 113, 123
inadvertent disclosure, 79–80
inference, 77–79
inflection, 106
influencing, 11, 28, 59, 60, 63, 65,
    123, 126
informational sentiments, 82, 86–87
intonation, 105

Key Messages, 35–37

lip-reading, 122

market, 11–12
Master of Persuasion (principles),
    125–128
Meeting Goal, 6–7, 25, 31, 47, 48,
    50, 52, 55, 57
  customer and supplier, 29–30
  customer's knowledge, 27–28
  perceptions, 28
  positioning, 29
  preparation, 26–27
  thinking, 25–26
  worksheet, 27
metaphors, 76

nervous speakers, 109–110
note and script-free, 110–111

online presentation, 116

padding, 68
Performance square, 14
personal appearance and setting, 123
persuasion, 1
  communication and, 3–4
  formula of, 4–5
  process of, 5–8, 125, 126
  sales process, 1–3
  See also Master of Persuasion
      (principles)
pitching and presentation, 7–8,
    97–98
  audience and, 99, 102
  body language, 118–120
  chat, 121–122
  conference and video call
      management, 116–118
  distractions, 103
  dramatic pause, 106–107
  engagement, 103–104
  flow seamlessly, 118
  hand gestures, 101
  inflection, 106
  intonation, 105

lip-reading, 122
  movement, 100–101
  nervous speakers, 109–110
  note and script-free, 110–111
  online, 116
  personal appearance and setting, 123
  pronunciation and clear speaking,
      122–123
  props, 101–102
  questions and answers, 120–121
  rehearsing, 111–115
  rhythm, 104–105
  Rule of Three, 107–108
  signposting, 108
  slides, 111
  video conferencing, 124
positioning, 29, 30
practice makes perfect, 112–113
presentation. See pitching and
      presentation
pronunciation, 122–123
props, 101–102

questions and answers, 120–121

rational thinking, 61–63, 65
regulation, 13
rehearsing, 112–113
request for proposal (RFP), 21–22, 45
Requirement Analysis Chart, 18–19
rhythm, 104–105
Rule of Three, 107–108

sales process, 1–3
sentiment, 80–83
signposting, 108
slides, 111
So What Test, 68–70
speaking, 60, 65, 99, 103–106,
      108–112, 116, 117, 122, 128
Story Plan, 7, 33, 40–41
  preparation, 34–35
  presentation structure, 38
  previous presentations, 37–38
  sentiment, 90–95
  thinking, 34
  Topic Running Order, 39–40

Topics for Discussion, 38–39
  worksheet, 35–37, 47, 49, 51, 53,
    55, 58
style and language, 7, 73–74
  aspirational sentiments, 85–86
  assertiveness, 74–75
  contextual sentiments, 83–84
  expositional sentiments, 87–89
  inadvertent disclosure, 79–80
  inference, 77–79
  informational sentiments, 86–87
  sentiment, 80–83
  simplification, 75–77
  Story Plan sentiment, 90–95

style block, 81–83; *See also* style and
  language

Three Cs, 66–68
Topic Running Order, 34–36,
  39–40
Topics for Discussion, 38–39

video call management, 116–118
video conferencing, 124
voice, 104
  inflection, 106
  intonation, 105
  rhythm, 104–105

OTHER TITLES IN THE CORPORATE COMMUNICATION COLLECTION

Debbie DuFrene, Stephen F. Austin State University, Editor

- *Fast Fulfillment* by Sanchoy Das
- *101 Tips for Improving Your Business Communication* by Edward Barr
- *Business Writing For Innovators and Change-Makers* by Dawn Henwood
- *Delivering Effective Virtual Presentations* by K. Virginia Hemby
- *New Insights into Prognostic Data Analytics in Corporate Communication* by Pragyan Rath and Kumari Shalini
- *Managerial Communication for Professional Development* by Reginald L. Bell and Jeanette S. Martin
- *Managerial Communication for Organizational Development* by Reginald L. Bell and Jeanette S. Martin
- *Business Report Guides* by Dorinda Clippinger
- *Strategic Thinking and Writing* by Michael Edmondson
- *Conducting Business Across Borders* by Adrian Wallwork
- *English Business Jargon and Slang Suzan* by St. Maur
- *Business Research Reporting* by Dorinda Clippinger
- *64 Surefire Strategies for Being Understood When Communicating with Co-Workers* by Walter St. John

Concise and Applied Business Books

The Collection listed above is one of 30 business subject collections that Business Expert Press has grown to make BEP a premiere publisher of print and digital books. Our concise and applied books are for...

- Professionals and Practitioners
- Faculty who adopt our books for courses
- Librarians who know that BEP's Digital Libraries are a unique way to offer students ebooks to download, not restricted with any digital rights management
- Executive Training Course Leaders
- Business Seminar Organizers

Business Expert Press books are for anyone who needs to dig deeper on business ideas, goals, and solutions to everyday problems. Whether one print book, one ebook, or buying a digital library of 110 ebooks, we remain the affordable and smart way to be business smart. For more information, please visit www.businessexpertpress.com, or contact sales@businessexpertpress.com.

Lightning Source UK Ltd.
Milton Keynes UK
UKHW020941021021
391556UK00005B/68